System Development

Springer

London
Berlin
Heidelberg
New York
Barcelona
Hong Kong
Milan
Paris
Singapore
Tokyo

Michael Bronzite

System Development

A Strategic Framework

Springer

Michael Bronzite, BSc, MSc, MBCS, CEng

ISBN 1-85233-176-3 Springer-Verlag London Berlin Heidelberg

British Library Cataloguing in Publication Data
Bronzite, Michael, 1936-
    System development : a strategic framework
    1.System design 2.Computer software - Development 3.Systems
    software - Management
    I.Title
    658.4'032
    ISBN 1852331763

Library of Congress Cataloging-in-Publication Data
A catalog record for this book is available from the Library of Congress

© Springer-Verlag London Limited 2000
Printed in Great Britain

Typesetting: Camera-ready by author
Printed and bound by the Athenæum Press Ltd., Gateshead, Tyne & Wear
34/3830-543210 Printed on acid-free paper SPIN 10724648

With much love, this book is dedicated to:

Joey Tycho

Kayla Tikvah

Nathan Arieh

Adam Jacques

There is the little known fairy story by Hans Christian Andersen. About the Emperor who was proud of his software systems. He was so proud of them that he announced that there would be a one day celebration with an enormous procession winding through his capital. The day dawned and all the major systems related to running the Empire – the administration, finance, the medical services, the fire and police departments – all the systems were represented in the procession. And every loyal subject lining the roadside was impressed and clapped and cheered as each float appeared on the route. All but one little system analyst. He looked and he looked and finally turned to his big departmental manager and said in a squeaky voice , "But, sir, hardly any of these systems are truly cost effective". "Sh, sh," said the burly departmental manager. But it was too late and everybody turned round to look at the system analyst who had dared to mention the unmentionable.

Perhaps it is only a fairy story.

And perhaps not.

This book is concerned with the development of software systems and the corporate framework needed to ensure success in that development. Why not dip in and find out for yourself?

MB   London 1999

Contents

Part 2	Into the abyss

Chapter 4   Analysis   53

Chapter 5   Planning   69

Part 3	Solving the problem

Chapter 8	**Taking stock**	125

Chapter 9	**The new approach - things**	135

Part 1 Setting the scene

What is your substance, whereof are you made,
That millions of strange shadows on you tend?

Sonnet 53, Shakespeare

Chapter 1 Introduction

Between $81 billion and $140 billion per year is wasted in the
United States alone on failed projects and overdue deliveries.

Chaos Report 1995 (The Standish Group)

The intent

The next hundred pages or so will offer you yet another discussion about
software systems and how to develop them. Much like scores of other books
on the shelves, perhaps. But this one is different.

All over the world, organisations are to be seen planning, developing,
designing, testing, installing, maintaining, upgrading and, ultimately, using
software systems. In turn, consultants, strategists, authors, and computer
magazine journalists, among others, analyse these systems and write up
progress reports on the system projects. And what is being suggested in most
of these reports is that the systems are ineffective, are not timely, and are
usually far from profitable.

Put another way, over the last thirty years or so, one simple premise stands
out:

The system development industry has consistently got it wrong.

Now these are brave words, and they may take some justification.
Nevertheless, the coming chapters will set out to validate this statement and
then move on to solve the implied problem.

What implied problem? At the simplest level, the problem can be summed
up by the short quotation printed at the top of this page. However bad the
inflation, eighty one billion dollars per annum (minimum) in the US is still not

a trivial amount of money. This is the annual sum reported to be wasted on software system projects. Projects that force companies into Chapter 11 administration. Projects that get cancelled before use. Projects that get the systems installed and then cancelled after use. Projects that do not get cancelled but the systems never work properly and the lawyers sharpen their pencils anyway. There has to be a logical explanation for all this. And there has to be a better way to plan and spend strategic budgets.

The overview

There will be many specific case studies scattered throughout the book, but to provide a simple example now, to give a view of the problem discussed above, consider the following report from roughly a decade ago.

> A survey published in 1990 revealed that a third of all computer projects in the UK ended up with an unusable product, or involving some form of serious overspend, i.e. a 'runaway' project. There were also reports that virtually all top US companies have suffered such runaway projects. As an example, the Allstate Insurance system was initially costed at $8 million in 1982 and, at the time of the survey, was planned to be installed in 1993 for about $100 million [1].

This type of development project, funded in this case by Allstate, is at the heart of this book. Note that it is not a technical issue – the problem is one of management, direction and competent decision-making at the top. The following pages describe a journey, taken over a number of years, to research the facts about system development and to find the underlying reasons for lack of success in this area. To explain why, in a world of ever accelerating change, the failure patterns of software system development have shown such a depressing constancy. The figures have not changed from the 1960s (see *Brooks* in the bibliography) to the end of the millennium (see *Glass* in the bibliography). The problem still exists today and still needs to be tackled. For this to be effective, there are three key steps to be taken:

Recognition   To accept that there is truly an issue here which, to date, is still without a solution. To establish beyond doubt that the majority of development programs for software systems continue to fail.

Understanding To diagnose the underlying root causes of these failure patterns. To identify the inherent mechanisms that lead most large long-term projects to exceed, say, project time estimates or budget allocations, or to not reach their target performance.

Correction   Finally, to apply significant changes to the strategic framework, corporate culture and management processes such as to take these mechanisms into account and to minimise their impact. These proposed changes will be fundamental and will tend to affect every corner of the corporation.

The book has been divided into three main parts, each of which will sensibly correspond to one of the functions discussed above.

❏   The first section (Chapters 1 to 3) will establish a baseline for the rest of the book. The approach will be to concentrate on large-scale projects and the methodology used in their development process. A number of surveys will be examined to show that the bulk of these projects do not succeed and this will be followed by some actual case studies which will reinforce the general pattern.

❏   The second section (Chapters 4 to 7) will dissect a number of key development processes to illustrate the underlying weakness and why the performance of current and past systems should cause no surprise. It will highlight the problem areas, the grey estimates and the low-probability assumptions that, up to the present, continue to determine the performance objectives and other goals of the system under development.

❏   Finally, in the third section (Chapters 8 to 12), recommendations will be put forward to change the organisation or its strategic direction. These recommendations will be specifically aimed to control and minimise the fault modes established in the earlier part of the book.

Note: for those with no time or patience to study the overall 'broad picture' view, Appendix 1 will offer senior management a fast-track 'cook-book' option, outlining the start of a strategic program that will ultimately enable the organisation to achieve good results. However, keep in mind that system development, much like good cooking, will still take a lot of effort, patience and training – and there is no short cut for good results.

In passing, the book itself has two main advantages: it is brief and it is non-technical. It is brief because it is focused on only one topic in the field of information technology – the development of software systems. It is non-technical because there are relatively few technical difficulties associated today with system development. As we shall see, the majority of problems in system development are generated from the non-technical side – in the strategic, the managerial, and the political arenas. All of these topics or viewpoints will be covered to some depth in later chapters.

Who should read this book? Well, for a start, anyone who lost some of that $81 billion in 1995. At least he or she will then know why. Perhaps some of the developers who helped to spend these huge amounts could also find it instructive. In addition, it is aimed squarely at today's strategic leaders, corporate planners, development and project administrators and end-user management. These are the guys who always end up signing on the line for their dream system of the future. Other potential readers will also include the current crop of MBA and graduate Information Technology students. Hopefully, they will soon be planning and authorising among themselves the next generation of commercial systems.

To summarise: the intent of this book is to explore the mechanics of software system development from a new vantage point and to identify why some of the standard processes are inherently failure-prone. Then, to go on to establish a practical set of rules or recommendations for development strategies which will significantly diminish the chance of costly failure. One potential impact is that it may call for a change of culture in the host organisation. In spite of the difficulties involved, this may be a price worth paying. Remember, the object is not to reduce the importance of engineering disciplines and skills, but to embed them into a more comprehensive and secure management environment.

A start-up test vehicle

You can, if you wish, take part in an experiment. Before getting into the body of the book, try to evaluate the following case history. Then, nearer the end of the book, we will take another look at the same problem and see how much, if at all, your views have changed. For this purpose, consider briefly the computer system 'Trawlerman':

> This development project with a suitable developer was approved by the UK Ministry of Defence in 1988. It was intended to provide an administrative system capable of handling classified information. At start-up, the date for operational delivery to the MOD was forecast to be 1991. In the event, hand-over did not occur until 1993 and the system

was not ready for operational use until 1995. At which point, the system was fully working, but it was deemed obsolete and the decision was made to scrap the whole exercise. The estimated cost of the development was in the region of £40 million. The key facts of this project came under the scrutiny of the Commons Public Accounts Committee in 1999 and they were not greatly impressed. The MOD said that valuable lessons had been learnt [2].

As we shall see in Chapters 2, 3 and elsewhere, this is a reasonably typical result in large-scale system development. Total time taken: 7 years; total cost: £40m; total value to the client: roughly nil. Now, assume you have top-level responsibility for this project – i.e. the equivalent managing director or CEO, but not the IT director – in the 1995 timeframe. The decision has just been made to scrap the entire project. What would you do at this point? Walk away? Set up and budget a completely new program? Ask the American and German governments what they are using? Spend about 10 minutes thinking about it and put down, say, 4 to 8 main proposals on how you would proceed in this situation given that the original need has not gone away. Put your proposal list to one side (or use it as a bookmark) and then we will take another look at this problem, and see how you might tackle it then, further into the book.

Structure and layout

The real work starts with Chapter 2, while the rest of this chapter has been given over to development basics. It has been put there to enable someone with absolutely no prior experience or knowledge of software systems, possibly some new clients or existing system users, to be able to read this book gainfully. The principal objective has been to make the book approachable to senior executives, managers and students with limited knowledge of Information Technology. On this basis, detailed technical material has been kept to an absolute minimum.

The references in the book – indicated in the text with square brackets [n] – will be found at the end of each chapter. The bibliography and document sections at the back of the book (which first list the title of the work, but which are nevertheless listed alphabetically by author) may also be found helpful in supplying supplementary sources of information. All dates are given in the UK notation, i.e. day/month/year. In addition to the rest of this chapter, Appendix 2 contains a number of basic explanations of some key concepts such as 'system' or 'failure' which are used in the book. Finally, note that there are two separate indexes: case studies and general topics.

The development life cycle

The life cycle is the basic planning format that has been applied to most development programs from the early days of software systems to the present time. It enables all the different organisational resources to be applied to the development process in an effective and timely manner. One variant of the SDLC model (System Development Life Cycle) is shown in Figure 1.1.

The activities flow from top-left to bottom-right, starting with 'Analysis'. Each activity can be recycled, as indicated by the small circular arrow in the bottom left-hand corner of each block, until some satisfactory result is obtained. The usual outcome is a body of work and a matching formal approved document. For the first activity, the analysis, this would be a review of any existing system or set of processes, followed by modifications to arrive at the proposed new system. This would lead to the distribution of the agreed deliverable, say, the 'Functional Specification', passed and approved by some supervisory body. This enables the next activity to be undertaken, i.e. the 'Design' phase, using the now-approved 'Functional Specification', as the driving reference. In other words, each of the activities shown in the Figure follows on sequentially from the previous one, ultimately delivering the next required reference document for use by the rest of the team. By the time the bottom right-hand corner has been reached, the entire system has been designed, tested, documented, installed and made operational. That is the theory, at any rate.

It is a popular approach and a quick glance at the model will show why it is attractive as a representation of the system development: it appears logical, sequential, and it will readily provide the basis for a structured management programme.

The life cycle shown in Figure 1.1 is important to the central argument of this book because most large system projects still use it or recommend it as a basis for their development planning. (A full-scale audit was carried out in the mid-90s on the systems development unit, the HIR, of the US House of Representatives. The audit report was critical of the methods and procedures in use, and strongly recommended the adoption of a formal SDLC methodology for all system development. The audit was thorough, professional, and clearly written, but the recommendation, I think, is a potential disaster. See what you think by the end of the book [3].) In order to become familiar with the SDLC, it is worth defining its individual elements in a little more detail:

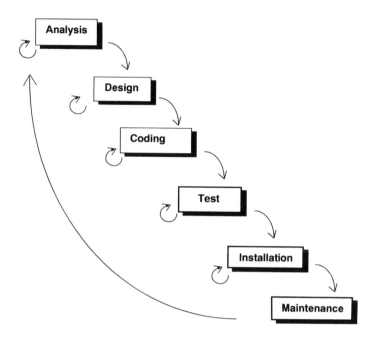

Figure 1.1 The development life cycle

Analysis

There are two main activities here. The first will involve a detailed examination of the previous system, whether verbal, paper-based or computerised. This data is then translated into a set of symbols on graphic drawings which will represent the model of how the old system works.

Design

Again two stages. First the 'logical design' is implemented. This is a process where every logical item defined in the analysis above is examined for ways to create more cost effectiveness, performance improvement, user friendliness, enhanced office automation, better compatibility with standards, extended facilities and so on. These new logical elements eventually become the basis for the new system. The 'physical design' then identifies the actual products, say, the data files to be used, screen layouts, report formats and so on. When all these physical elements are eventually assembled and installed on the client's site, they will form the new working system.

Coding

The formal programming section where the actual system instructions are prepared. These instructions, based on the logical design criteria, will conform to the grammar and syntax of the selected programming language.

Test

The process where sub-routines, blocks of software and, eventually, entire systems are subjected to a set of simulated real-life test sequences to check for a) obvious errors of design, and b) conformance to the original system specifications in terms of operations and performance.

Installation

The transference of the finished system from the developer's test-bed conditions to the client's operational environment.

Maintenance

All the additional work on the system that is carried out after hand-over. This may include error-fixing, adding extra features, or full performance upgrades (see Appendix 2). Regardless, each maintenance activity is seen as a system redesign which will call for a whole new life cycle of activity (Figure 1.1).

The life cycle is not used as a planning tool by itself, but it is an important conceptual part of a number of methodologies (Appendix 2) which are used as planning tools. Popular examples of such methodologies include SSADM (Great Britain), Merise (France), and YSM (United States) [4]. We will have reason to re-examine aspects of this life cycle and its impact later in the book.

The role in the organisation

The life cycle shows where each development phase fits into the stream of planned activities necessary to produce an operating administration system. But this is obviously not the total picture in terms of the way the organisation interacts with system related work, and this is outlined below in Figure 1.2. It illustrates the various factors that can affect the implementation of each phase of the development activity. Take, for example, the technical team working to satisfy the original performance specification. Now consider all the individual elements that (sometimes for the best possible reasons) are likely to impede them from reaching their objectives.

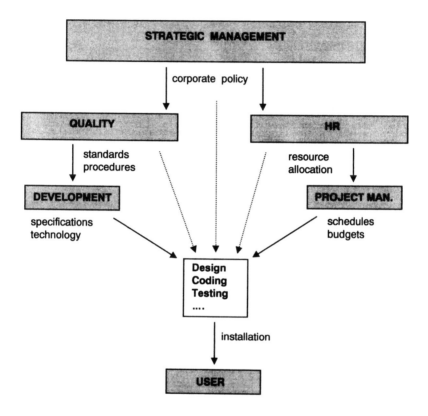

Figure 1.2   The pressures on development

User

As the development cycle progresses, the user may well insist on changes to the overall specification or implementation. This will be to make the actual system better suited to the organisation's environment or to better match the user's new perceptions of need.

Development

To meet the requirements laid down in the specification, the development team will be forced to work with the analysis tools, programming language, debugging software, hardware platform and test facilities provided by the department which is employing the programmers. None of these may be necessarily optimum.

Project Management

The actual start and stop times, the major milestones for this exercise, along with the size and scope (and work related stress) of the team will all be designated by this department and will be strongly dependent on budget limits set, perhaps, one or two years ago. It is not the norm for enough time or resource to be allocated.

Quality

This will set down the accepted standards for design where, for example, the requirements related to commercial aircraft software may well be more stringent than those for an application package in the office. The implications for development could be related to the documentation, style of programming, acceptance procedures, change controls and nature of the test programme. All of this could significantly add to the development burden and, indirectly, cause delay in the final delivery.

HR

The Human Resource department will be responsible for assigning the number and quality of personnel to the team, providing for their working conditions, training programs, as well as handling the day to day personnel problems. Their strategies and priorities may not necessarily match the objectives of the development team.

Strategic Management

The system priorities, much like all other corporate activities, will be subject to, and controlled by, the changing strategic objectives of the organisation.

We have not gone into any great detail on how these different sections of the organisation can impact the overall progress of the project. For all that, it should be clear how they could possibly interfere with and frustrate a given system development. And there are other potential problem areas. For example, any of the following could prove difficult to handle:

Specifications   If the original specification is not realistic or achievable then all the work in the world will not deliver a workable system. This is not such an unusual situation: examples will be seen in Chapter 3 while the whole topic will be treated in more detail in Chapter 4.

Procedures   The scope, nature and delivery of, say, an over-detailed corporate documentation plan can radically affect the overall workload of the development team.

Inter-working   Development is primarily a group or social interaction activity. Large projects tend to have large teams (or sets of teams). If there is not a good rapport between the individuals of a team or between the teams themselves then the needed co-operation just will not occur.

Personal   It seems that people in their thirties - to say nothing of twenties or forties - still go in for pregnancies, job changes, affairs, house purchases, and divorces (although not necessarily in that order). These are common enough activities, but any one of them could have a severe impact on the development team's capabilities.

Summary

❑ This book will seek to address the issue of current software system development as a continuing high cost and poor success-rate product – independent of location.

❑ Large, long time-scale system development exercises are still based today on the classic life cycle model SDLC.

❑ The activities of the life cycle can be impaired by damaging inputs – either internally from the other sections of the organisation or based on unanticipated external changes.

References

1 Flood G, 'Runaway' projects affect 60%, *Computer Weekly*, 8.3.90, p. 3

2 Shaw D, £40m storm over Ministry computer that was never used, *London Evening Standard*, 16.6.99, p.27

3 Report no. 95-CAO-20, The House needs to follow a structured approach…, www.house.gov/IG/95cao20/report.htm

4 Avison D, and Fitzgerald G, Information Systems Development: Methodologies, Techniques and Tools, McGraw Hill, 1995

Chapter 2 Formulating the problem

Philosophy

In the first instance, is there truly a problem out there? Are systems still failing? In answer to that, the next few pages will constitute a sales pitch with a clear objective – I want you to buy into the following premise:

For large-scale software system development, failure is the norm.

In other words, failure is the only reasonable expectation for this sort of activity. Now this is not exactly the standard message to be found in most serious textbooks. So the approach will be to travel slowly and carefully. Note that there will be no effort at this stage to explain why the premise should be so and, further, there will be no provision of work-rounds or solutions. Once the argument has been accepted, then these tasks can be explored, later, in Parts 2 and 3 of the book. The sole object of this chapter is to convince you that the Emperor, if you will it, has no clothes.

How will this be done? The strategy will be to provide you with suitable data. You will then judge for yourself if the sources are professional and if the broad totality of the presented data is consistent. If it is taken from enough sources, and if its main conclusions can be accepted, then this data will be used to assess the validity of the above premise.

So let the convincing begin.

Reports, surveys and summaries

We can get started with a small appetiser...

Data warehousing

This is a business application that has been one of the key driving technologies of the 90s. It is essentially a high performance database system. It offers the possibility of generating enormous amounts of data and then accurately querying that data for precise details about, say, the habits and preferences of a client in a supermarket environment ('data mining'). The investment is considerable, the learning curve is steep and the demand on the company culture is also significant. And one or two highly publicised successful examples have become beacons for the rest of the crowd. The hype has been extensive and virtually all commercial organisations of any size will have seriously considered going down this route. With growing popularity, the professional studies have appeared, the 'how-to' books were published and the magazines prepared extensive supplements on every aspect of the subject [1].

Then the first rumblings appeared. To be followed by surveys. Such as the one by Organisation and Technology Research (OTR) which appeared early in 1997 ('Do the Benefits of Data Warehousing Justify the Costs?'). This one looked at roughly 1500 European companies and found that hardly any of them received any ROI (return on investment) from their data warehouse investment [2].

This was followed by further independent surveys, including the one by Druid Research for the Data Warehouse Network. This addressed 280 European users and found that 65% of them had warehousing projects in the pipeline. It further established that roughly 60% of these projects were failing [3].

Are we talking only about Europe? As an aside given in a magazine interview, a successful businesswoman in the US (voted 'Entrepreneur of the Year' in 1993) indicated that about 50% of all warehouse projects could be expected to fail [4].

As potential learning material, it would obviously be helpful to have a case study outline or a description of the processes that can lead to project problems in this area. And there is one - names very properly changed - but fully researched all the same. It concerns a services company and a project that was undertaken through 1996 to provide data warehousing capabilities. About a year after start-up, the project was finally cancelled for an overall cost of about $750 thousand [5].

Now imagine for the moment that you and your partner have finally decided to purchase a house in a nice part of town. The cost will nearly break you but the eventual advantage of ownership will certainly make the whole exercise worth while. You are about to sign the contract for the selected house when your surveyor points that there is a 50% chance of serious subsidence in the immediate area. If proven, this would reduce the value of the house to zero. You cannot take insurance against the possibility and the surveyor will not be held responsible. Question : would you take the chance and invest your life savings in that house?

This is pretty much the equivalent situation if the data warehouse examples given above are valid. Data warehousing *is* an important commercial tool and it *can* give a sound competitive advantage. But, if there is evidence that the considerable effort and investment involved could be wasted, then it is surely prudent to move with due care and to set up damage limitation procedures. Or, perhaps, to look for alternative investments with a better chance of success.

Data warehousing is not unique. Had we selected Business Process Re-engineering (BPR), for example, we could have shown a similar pattern of initial enthusiasm followed by the growing recognition of some of the disadvantages that come with the process [6]. This section on data warehouses has been used purely as an introductory example, not an in-depth study. It has, however, illustrated how surveys are more likely to provide reliable information than a single instance report - especially if that dedicated report is sourced by a product supplier with vested interests. It has also indicated that *repeated* surveys which broadly agree in general outline (ideally carried out by different organisations, at different times and in different locations) must generate considerably more confidence in the conclusions than any single set of figures.

With that in mind, we can now move on to some professional surveys based on the more general analysis of software system development, all carried out through the 90s in different countries and presented here in chronological order.

The Kearney report [7]

Source	A.T.Kearney, founded over 70 years ago. It is a large management consulting organisation with offices located in 58 cities in 34 countries in the Americas, Africa, Asia Pacific and Europe.
Publication date	1990
Location	London UK Tel: 0207 468 8000
Objective	To assess the effectiveness of IT application in the UK
Size of sample	3500 questionnaires sent; 400+ returned filled in
Respondents	Board level users across widely varying businesses
Success rate	11%
Comment	The original figure for successful development and application of IT systems from the companies themselves was nearer 65%. The low figure quoted here was based on a more objective model defined by Kearney which addressed areas of corporate culture, impact and effectivity (Figure 11 in the report). The companies' own assessment was usually too optimistic.

The Pagoda report [8]

Source	Pagoda Consulting Ltd. As management consultants based in the UK, operating with a global reach, Pagoda help a wide range of blue chip clients to optimise the use of technology to deliver business benefit.
Publication date	1994
Location	London UK Tel: 0207 436 9464
Objective	To establish why systems fail to deliver
Size of sample	About 100 organisations were studied for a year with further interviews and follow-ups conducted with about 30 of those companies.
Respondents	-

Success rate   11%

Comment   The emphasis is on studying the impact of change on the
                    organisation and the report highlights some surprising
                    conclusions. Such as the lack of correlation between IT
                    investment and business benefit. Again, 89% of
                    application projects in the UK were considered not fully
                    successful.

The Standish Group report [9]

Source   The Standish Group International Inc. is a US market
                    research and advisory firm specialising in mission critical
                    software.

Publication date   1995

Location   Dennis, Mass, US   Tel : (508) 385 7500

Objective   To establish the scope of project failures and to identify
                    the major factors that are responsible.

Size of sample   365 surveys returned

Respondents   American IT executive managers

Success rate   (% of companies with projects on time and on budget)

                    Large   9%

                    Medium 16%

                    Small   28%

Comment   The survey appears to have been very thorough and
                    professionally handled. The results generated are fairly
                    depressing, but are fully in line with the individual
                    comments elicited by the extended focus groups, set up
                    to discuss failure modes, in both Boston and San
                    Francisco.

The PricewaterhouseCoopers report [10]

Source   PricewaterhouseCoopers is a global provider of
                    accounting, auditing, tax and consulting services. The
                    company has offices in more than 120 countries.

Publication date	1996
Location	London UK Tel : 0207 939 3000
Objective	To establish what proportion of organisations had experienced major problems with computer systems.
Size of sample	A total of 536 large companies located in North America, Europe and Singapore.
Respondents	Directors and senior managers
Success rate	Over the previous two years, 60% of all organisations sampled had suffered a serious system project failure. In addition, 35% of organisations had experienced a major control failure with an operational system. (Of the project failures, 23% of them had caused serious financial loss to the organisation.)
Comment	The survey was not geared to establishing a simple measure of success or failure for each project. Rather, it had identified a number of failure mechanisms and studied the impact of these mechanisms across the sample group. Although differently structured, the report will still make interesting reading for someone about to embark on a new investment in this area.

The OASIG report [11]

Source	OASIG is a special interest group supported by the DTI. It is concerned with the human and organisational aspects of Information Technology and promoting action in those areas.
Publication date	1996
Location	Sheffield UK Tel : (0) 114 222 3229
Objective	To examine the levels of performance of IT projects and the role played by human, organisational and managerial factors.
Size of sample	45

Respondents	Leading UK researchers and consultants (drawing on collective experiences from 14000 user organisations)
Success rate	10 to 20% (average input)
Comment	This is an interesting approach in that the end user is not directly addressed. The inputs themselves come from experts in the system development field. This implies that a) they can call on a huge collective experience pool derived from many sources, b) they are competent to assess the damage and c) there will be less chance of 'forgetting' embarrassing projects. For all the differences, the results are basically in line with all the other surveys.

The KPMG report [12]

Source	KPMG's Strategic and Technology Group. This management consultancy group applies IT techniques to assist and improve the competitive position of its clients situated in Canada. In this capacity, it can additionally call on the full resources of other offices of KPMG International.
Publication date	1997
Location	Toronto Canada Tel : (416) 777 3482
Objective	To establish the key reasons why IT systems projects continue to fail.
Size of sample	1450 questionnaires sent; 176 returned and used
Respondents	Canadian chief executives
Success rate	Comparable to the Standish report.
Comment	The main objective was to determine the common sources of failure in IT projects. (It is worth noting that failures due to unplanned changes were not included in the final results.) This target was largely achieved (e.g. the principal reason for failure was claimed to be poor project planning - identified by 73% of respondents).

These findings were backed up by the actual comments from the respondents.

Summary of results

The above data represents a significant input in assessing how successfully government, science, commerce and industry have specified and applied software systems in the 90s. The key parameters have been summarised in the table below:

Table 2.1 Summary of survey results

Location	Year	Source	No. Samples	Success Rate (%)
London, UK	1990	Kearney	400	11
London, UK	1994	Pagoda	100	11
Dennis, USA *	1995	Standish - small	365	28
	1995	Standish - medium		16
	1995	Standish - large		9
Sheffield, UK **	1996	OASIG	45	15
Toronto, Canada	1997	KPMG	176	16

Overall Total samples	1086
Overall Average Success Rate (%)	15

*   total no. of samples for all three types

**   reported success rate between 10 and 20%

It is worth highlighting the critical points of Table 2.1.

❏ There are 7 'success' inputs (even if 3 came from a single source);

❏ The data was extracted from experience gained in three countries;.

❏ The time span has stretched out over the last 7 years;

❏ The surveys were planned and carried out by 5 different sources.

Another way of looking at the established key data is via a combined graphical format:

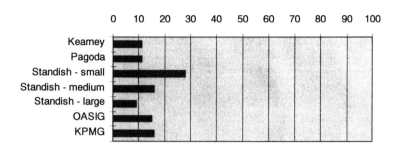

Figure 2.1   The success rate (%) from the surveys

And by now, the key conclusion should be inescapable (and this more or less gets us back to the premise at the start of the chapter) :

❏ Consolidating data from all the surveys, the expectation of success when planning conventional software system development will be sensibly constant (and sensibly low).

This simple statement appears to be both valid and totally unacceptable as a measure of the output from an established engineering discipline. It is the driving justification for the rest of the book.

Reasons for failure

Another difficult area. At the outset it was stated that this chapter would not discuss reasons for failure. This is largely true in that it will not discuss reasons that *I* think are insightful or lead to a useful understanding of failure mechanisms. For that, go to Part 2 of the book. This section will, however, offer the 'traditional' view of failure which has been well studied and reviewed in the reports. Why do I promote these surveys for the actual failure statistics while minimising the significance of the reasons put forward? Once again, it is a matter of outlook. Consider a typical road accident.

The motorway accident model

It is seven o'clock on a damp, misty, winter morning on the motorway. One van has a puncture on a bad bend just outside the local town. One minute later, 34 vehicles are severely damaged, 9 people are dead, and 32 others are severely injured and will require hospital treatments of varying complexity. The motorway is shut down in one direction for the entire day and the other direction suffers severe hold-ups as the drivers slow down to view the carnage.

Now one can physically count the vehicles, bodies and injured victims. No ambiguity there. With more difficulty, one can fairly estimate the cost of the public and medical services, the hospital facilities and the transport loss of the major road link for the day.

But now look at the possible range of causes. One simple set of reasons for the accident could be:

❏ The van was poorly maintained;

❏ Drivers were not driving within their limits of visibility;

❏ Weather conditions were treacherous;

❏ Early morning is a bad time of day to estimate distances.

These are explicit and very likely legitimate reasons. But there could be another, more community-based, view of the pile-up resulting in a totally different set of causes :

❏ The under-funded police could not fully man the motorway patrol;

❏ The local council chose not to install an effective warning system;

❏ The law does not call for adequate tests on commercial vehicles;

❏ The government will not fund a campaign for better driving habits.

Notice how the second set of explanations for the accident are, in a number of ways, more useful than the first, in that they can point to possible corrective action that can be undertaken if there is a will to take such action. With enough money, for example, you can install a signalling system or an advertising campaign to improve the driving culture. However, virtually unlimited funding will do very little in terms of improving the weather.

In short, returning now to software systems, it is fairly easy to count the actual number of failures in a given software package. All that is required is a good test specification. It is more open to question when specific reasons are put forward to explain those failures. For all that, it will be useful to compare the conventional approach to analysing system failure with the material contained in Part 2. Once again, you will have to be the judge of the relative merits of these two sets of data.

Reported causes of failure in system development

Of the six survey sources given in Table 2.1 above, five gave a lot of effort to identifying the failure patterns. A summary of main reasons are:

Kearney   User requirement, Management support, User involvement, Teamwork

Standish   User requirement, User involvement, Spec changes, Tech. incompetence

PWCoopers User requirement, Project planning, Accountability, Poor reporting

OASIG   User requirement, Business case, User involvement, Project planning, Tech. incompetence

KPMG   User requirement, Business case, Management support, Project planning, Tech. Incompetence

Once again, this can be shown graphically, the failure cause shown on the y axis and the frequency of occurrence given along the x axis:

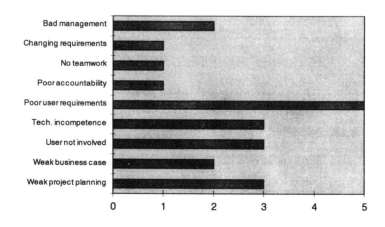

Figure 2.2   The principal reasons given for project failures

There is little of surprise here, although Figure 2.2 strongly indicates just how important user requirements can be. It has a value of '5' in the plot because all five of the quoted surveys indicated that inadequate user requirement specifications was a significant factor in the failure process.

Assessment

For those in denial, there is always the sneaky feeling that the survey results were in some way massaged or only carefully pre-selected data used. Or that the market researchers only used chosen respondents from some full range. Two points in response :

❑ Try some other surveys not covered above. Look at the non-positive way business managers regard the IT department [13]. Or the fact that most users do not appear to succeed in their use of IT [14]. Or the 'rare' inclusion of IT in the strategic planning by the majority of multinational companies responding to another questionnaire [15];

❑ On a completely different tack, the sources of these surveys are large global consultants. Collective bias from such groups is somewhat unlikely.

By now, the consensus has to be that you have a 10 to 20% chance of injecting money into a new system project and getting back the system defined in the functional specification for the time and cost estimates given in the contract.

So why carry on?

❑ You did not know how badly the cards were stacked;

❑ Your software team is the one in six that is project competent;

❑ You are a natural born optimist;

❑ What choice does your company have? You need the systems.

Of which, only the last excuse is probably reasonable. IT is a strategic weapon that tends to be intensively applied in most corporate environments. As such, failure is just another problem in the scheme of things that will have to be addressed - and overcome.

We will continue to explore this problem in the next chapter. Some case histories will be analysed to illustrate further just what is meant by a failed project and to reveal some of the key features that can lead up to this unfortunate condition.

Summary

❑ It is a central assumption of this chapter that if a group of professional surveys reach the same conclusion, there is a very strong likelihood that the conclusion is valid.

❑ A number of surveys on the subject of failure related to software system development were reviewed. They had slightly varied formats, were carried out over a number of years, were located in different countries and came from six different sources.

❑ The surveys showed a remarkable agreement over the principal conclusion - that any new software development project stood about a 10 to 20% chance of success. And no more.

What is of particular interest is how reports of project failure have continued to be written over the last three decades - virtually without change. Whatever has been done up to now has clearly failed to show any radical improvement in the success rate of software development - certainly for the larger projects.

References

1 Data Warehousing Supplement, *Computer Weekly*, 30.5.1996

2 Vowler J, Has data warehousing had its day?, *Computer Weekly*, 27.2.1997, p.36

3 Kelly S, Warehousing projects fail to make the grade, *Computing*, 27.11.1997, p.28

4 The business end - interview with Dr Kay Hammer, *Information Age*, Feb/Mar 1998, p.16

5 Paul L, Anatomy of a Failure : Data Warehousing, CIO Enterprise, 15.11.1997

6 Hayward D, Facing the firing squad, Computing, 2.11.1995, p.36

7 Kearney AT, Breaking the Barriers - IT Effectiveness in Great Britain and Ireland, (see under *Documents*)

8 Pagoda Consulting, Understanding why systems fail to deliver, (see under *Documents*)

9 The Standish Group, Chaos – Application Project and Failure, (see under *Documents*)

10 PricewaterhouseCoopers, Managing information and systems risks, (see under *Documents*)

11 OASIG, The Performance of Information Technology and the Role of Human and Organisational Factors, (see under *Documents*)

12 KPMG, What went wrong? Unsuccessful Information Technology Projects, (see under *Documents*)

13 Boyle B, Report shows that IT is a mystery to most business managers, *Computer Weekly*, 22.6.95, p.3

14 Researchers blow myth of competitive advantage, *Computing*, 1.11.90, p.4

15 Harvey D, IT is still an afterthought for business planners, *Computer Weekly*, 8.8.91, p.8

Chapter 3   Patterns of development

Introduction

The review of available data in Chapter 2 established an average failure rate for software system development at about 85%. This was based on figures generated over the last decade from a variety of sources.

This chapter will continue the analytical process by examining a number of associated case studies. The intent is to identify some of the common properties and underlying reasons for the poor results. It is worth keeping in mind that the following case histories tend to involve fully-qualified engineers, competent project teams, successful organisations, and all this coupled with a determination to succeed by all the related parties.

By way of an entry into the problem area we can examine a relatively classic model, even though it is not based on an IT development.

The British Library

The leading characteristic of this exercise was the excessive gestation period which caused a whole set of unexpected problems to arise, thereby adding to the general delay. It also gives an interesting insight into the workings of central government and the processes involved in co-operating with local government. It essentially breaks down into two separate phases.

Phase I (Planning)

1951   The County of London Development Plan was the first
       document to identify a new library space on the existing site by
       the British Museum in Bloomsbury.

1955   The local council insisted that another site be found.

1962   The local council reluctantly agreed the existing site.

1967   Following ongoing representations from the new local council
       (due to the 1965 reorganisation of London government) the
       government agreed not to pursue the previously selected
       Bloomsbury site.

1970   A government White Paper proposed that the library should be
       built on the original Bloomsbury site.

1971   The Greater London Council (GLC) and the local council
       agreed that a new site near Kings Cross should be investigated.

1974   The new Labour government supported the Kings Cross site.

1975   Agreement was reached by all parties that the Kings Cross site
       would be acceptable. (Twenty four years after the first plan
       was put forward.)

1978   The Secretary for Education and Science announced that the
       first phase of the overall project would be built over the period
       1979/1989 for a cost of about £75 million. But that was not to
       be the end of the construction. There were to be, in all, three
       phases which would be completed in 1999. At this point, the
       new site would provide space for 3,500 readers and 23 million
       books [1].

It is of interest that [1] defined this project as a 'near-disaster' because it
had initially been something of a music-hall joke with the ever elastic
decision-making processes and scheduling targets. But, said the book when
first published in 1980, the project had more or less turned itself round and
was more or less back on track (after only 27 years). So let's see how it all
turned out.

Phase II (Implementation)

1994   The new computerised book catalogue was found to be highly
       unreliable while the old printed catalogue had been removed
       and was no longer available on-site [2].

1995   Delivery dates and cost figures continued to be extended on a regular basis. Some of the errors were so bad that questions were raised about the possibility of deliberate sabotage [3]. Problems included :
- Moveable shelving jammed. It had to be replaced;
- The installed air conditioning was found to be unsuitable;
- Thousands of miles of defective wiring had to be changed;
- The ceiling was too low, it had to be taken down and rebuilt at the required level.

1996   National Audit Office published an official report (but only after the contents were vetted by the Secretary of State for National Heritage) [4]. Main points raised :
- Expected completion now slipped to October 1996;
- Cash limits raised in 1994 from £450 to £496 million;
- Prior to 1991 the quality aspects were inadequate;
- Capacity in Science and Oriental rooms would be exceeded at opening.

1997   Cost had now risen to £511 million. Formal opening planned to be in November 1997, but the building will not be completed by then [5].

Not bad for one 'near disaster'. By the end of the decade, the library was (more or less) open and functioning. Taken from my personal viewpoint, it has a beautiful interior, mixing cool functionality with elegant style. But nothing to warrant the more than 25 years of disputes, inept management, incompetence and ever-rising costs.

All the case studies described in here and in the following pages have been selected (from a very large parent population) simply to underscore the general statistics given in the last Chapter. Another reason will be to look for any basic patterns that can be seen repeatedly in project after project. In this case, the sad litany of one UK government project management exercise can be analysed to look for any important or useful features. In fact, there are two points of general interest here, let's call them rules of conduct :

Rule 1   When there is no clearly defined accountable authority for a project, then progress, performance, and client satisfaction are not likely to be particularly relevent parameters for that project;

Rule 2   When someone else's money is being spent, the amount of money being spent is largely unimportant.

Central government

We will take a brief look at just one department in the United Kingdom as sufficient for our purposes. The selected body (from many possible candidates) is the Department of Social Security and it has had three important development programs over the last two decades which are worth more than the occasional glance. The first was probably the most advanced and ambitious:

Operational Strategy

This was a development that came from poor but honest parentage – the previous project CAMELOT. The honesty came from the start-up intent in the 70s while the poverty lay in the eventual results obtained in 1982 when CAMELOT was finally laid to rest for a total loss of about £6 million. In 1984 the wholly new state-of-the-art system replacement was launched with all the promise and fanfare of the early Thatcher period. This particular system (ominously claimed to be the 'biggest in Europe') was going to control benefit payments in the UK. At the time, the department was known as the DHSS (Department of Health and Social Security), and the project was given the acronym LOMP (Local Office Microcomputer Project) until it devolved into the altogether more grandiose and exciting 'Operational Strategy'. At the time, the overall cost was estimated to be about £700 million and this outlay was going to be fully recovered from the loss of 20,000 jobs. That was the plan, anyway.

1988   The cost had somehow risen by an additional £500 million, but the current parliamentary secretary was still able to describe the LOMP as a 'magnificent achievement'. However the original planned savings of £1.1 billion was looking less probable [6].

1989   The cost figure reported to the House of Commons had risen to £1.7 billion, but the DSS now suggested that this figure could go to £2 billion. At the same time, the staff were protesting at the loss (!) in office efficiency that resulted from using the system [7].

1991   Various claims relating to pensions and income support were not being processed adequately and the MP concerned was being flooded with complaints. The DSS, in reply, did not feel that there was a serious problem [8].

1994   The overall cost had now risen to £2.6 billion. A spokeswoman for the DSS claimed that the system had already made a saving of over £3 billion, but was unable to give details. (The previous year yet another senior civil servant had been able to describe the project as a 'remarkable success'.) [9] A more extensive analysis of the project suggested that the project risk levels were too high, that the DSS lacked professional project experience, that industrial relations were poor and that the tight deadlines were unrealistic. Additionally, Social Security reforms introduced in the mid-80s caused a significant additional workload to the project due to changing requirements [10].

1996   The original justification of the whole project was the anticipated reduction of jobs from the DSS payroll which would in effect cover the development costs (initially planned at £700 million). It now transpired that, not only had the development costs increased by about 350% from the original estimate, but – far from the targeted 20,000 job losses – the number of staff had actually *increased* by over 1000 from the original 1989 figures [11].

The only pragmatic conclusion is that this department probably spent about £2.5 billion on 'Operational Strategy' for not very much in return. And this lack of results was not occurring in a vacuum. Consider the parties involved:

Parliament   There were repeated, public criticisms from MPs, appropriate committees and the National Audit Office.

End-users   A number of strikes and walk-outs by DSS employees were related to poor operational efficiency and increased workload.

'Clients'   The benefit claimants complained regularly of suffering from omissions, delays, errors and poor turnaround.

And still the project lumbered on. Anything new to learn from the experience? Well, clearly, the rules proposed in the previous section apply here. Additionally –

Rule 3   If a new project is declared 'complex and challenging' or the equivalent, it is very unlikely to succeed the first time round.

ASSIST

ASSIST (Analytical Services Statistical Information System) was primarily intended as a data feeder system for the DSS ministers when having to answer searching or obscure questions by the parliamentary opposition or the media. The original plan was that the fixed price for the project would be in the approximate range £25 million and the contract, which was signed with the developers in January 1993, would include maintenance for a number of years after installation. The deliverables were fully defined: the first phase to be completed by year-end 1993, phase II by September 1994 and the final phase by July 1995 [12]. This was again a fairly tight schedule, but hope springs eternal...

> 1994   Eight months into the project there was a reported slippage of 4 months, software error levels remained high and the overall cost estimates had risen to about £50 million. A spokesman for the project admitted that it was a complex system [13].

> 1995   ASSIST collapsed near the end of 1994. A spokesman for the DSS said that it might now be developed in-house or with the assistance of another supplier. Another member of the DSS established that there were no plans to re-use this system. More to the point, the DSS had broken with tradition, and brought a legal action against the developers to recover monies already paid out [14].

> 1997   An out-of-court settlement was finally agreed between the DSS and the developers of the cancelled project ASSIST. Details were kept confidential, but a) the DSS publicly expressed satisfaction with the result, b) no admission of blame from any party was made and c) media reports suggested that no compensation was ever recovered by the DSS. On the contrary, it was suggested that the unfortunate DSS would have to pay outstanding legal costs of more than £1 million [15].

At one level, this is simply another relatively modest mis-handled project funded by the public purse. However, what makes it a little bit different is the novel action of the department concerned in seeking redress through the courts. Dispute management will be discussed in more detail in Chapter 7, but here the sole result seems to have been the penalty of additional legal costs to be covered by the innocent taxpayer.

National Insurance Recording System 2 (Nirs2)

Nirs2 was yet another of those carefully negotiated projects intended to provide an automated benefits calculation and payment system for one arm of the DSS, the Contributions Agency. In April 1995, the contract was signed with the objective of replacing the current Nirs1 by Spring 1997. Ongoing extensions would then be added over the following 2 years. It was going to be a large system and it was going to be specifically needed to meet the requirements of the new pensions regulations of 1997. It was also one of the first contracts to involve a PFI (the government's Private Finance Initiative – a project concept where someone other than the Treasury is responsible for covering the development costs).

1996   By April of this year, the contract had been re-negotiated to enable the developer to extend the timetable. With Andersen agreeing to pay back some fees, the new system would begin to replace the existing software in Spring 1997 with the whole exercise planned to be completed some time in 1999 [16].

1997   The National Audit Office gave a largely positive review of Nirs2. The overall cost was declared at some £135 million and the NAO felt the project provided good value for money. In particular it recommended the contractual details as a possible model for other Government contracts [17].

1999   The system eventually went operational in July 1998, some 18 months later than planned. For all that, by April of 1999 – 10 months later still, the data available for processing was still not comprehensive or trustworthy. Additionally, what was a little worrying was the statement from one DSS official that all the developed systems of the 80s should now be considered as obsolescent and ready for replacement [18]. In June of the same year, the Public Accounts Committee (a governmental review body) criticised the developers who, in turn, put the blame on the people filling in the National Insurance forms incorrectly – estimated at just under a third of the total. What was a little more depressing was the statement that the developer apparently had an adversarial relationship with the client – who, themselves, had changed ownership during the project from the DSS to the Treasury [19].

Overview

These three projects covered roughly the two decades 80s and 90s, all sourced from the same department of central government. The summary overview could be generally applied to any large government project:

❏ Little appears to have been learnt in terms of experience carried over from one generation of system development to the next;

❏ Each new project is launched full of optimism and confidence;

❏ At termination, each new project has generally under-performed and over-spent by a healthy margin;

❏ The relationship between the client and the developer tends to deteriorate during the lifetime of the project.

Military systems

There are usually special considerations related to military applications. They demand secure confidential networks, ultra-reliable operations, and standards for long-life capability in a non-benign environment. Nevertheless, having studied the preceding sections, the following example may yet generate a certain sense of *déjà vu...*

Corporate Head Office Technology System (CHOTS)

There was a need (rest assured, there is *always* a need) to replace a number of disparate office systems with one comprehensive inter-linking approach to office automation. In this case, the UK Ministry of Defence proposed a project (CHOTS) to provide suitable computer applications for all its main offices in the UK. The idea, first put forward in 1984, called for the development of a £250 million Unix-based system operating on 10,000 terminals. Needless to say, CHOTS was claimed to be the largest and most complex secure office automation project in Europe.

> 1988   Four years into the program the two opposed views were already much in evidence. On the one hand, the House of Commons select committee considered that the project was a complete waste of time and that effort was being spent in trying to re-invent the wheel. Furthermore, a wheel that was

not wanted by any of the users. On the other hand, the project manager was not aware of any criticisms [20].

1991 British Telecom (BT) formally dropped out of the bidding (seven years after the project was first proposed) leaving only one contender (ICL) for the project [21].

1992 The House of Commons Public Accounts Committee severely criticised the MoD after 8 out of 9 projects were reported to be in difficulties. Better project management and quality control were recommended. The report also commented on the MoD's showing in the £500 million CHOTS project [22].

1995 There had been further criticism from the users that the system, while operational, was cumbersome and 'old-fashioned' (i.e. based on a Unix command-line interface). In an effort to make the product more user-friendly, the MoD planned to upgrade the program to make it compatible with Windows 3.11 – which itself had already been replaced for some time by Windows95. This upgrade would bring the system cost up to about £400 million. However users continued to comment that the bulk of their e-mail communications (90%) were unclassified so the extra security, and corresponding application complexity, was simply not required [23].

1996 The MoD now plans to replace the Unix operating system with Windows NT on the server and Microsoft Office on the client machines. In August 1996, the first office went live with a Windows 3.11 implementation [24].

This was a relatively unusual project in that it was more or less successful. It was planned and developed, difficulties were overcome, ICL delivered it (eventually) and it worked. But there was one small nagging problem – at no time did the end-users ever express any real interest in using CHOTS. The design authority was obsessed with security while the users just wanted the convenience of using standard application packages. On a different tack, observe how the cost of the exercise kept changing. One wonders just how accurately the costs were controlled or reported. Again, notice how a long development life-cycle (much like the 'Operational Strategy' project) had to be extended again and again to accommodate the technical improvements and unexpected changes that occurred with time. These changes severely impacted the potential success of the project. Which leads to the general conclusions:

Rule 4   Any system that is not wanted by the user – is not wanted;

Rule 5   The planning schedule for any project which starts off long will always get a great deal longer.

Financial systems

There is one over-riding reason why system failure rates in financial institutions are hard to determine : in an area where reputation and financial probity are considered all-important, no-one wishes to admit responsibility for such public errors of judgement or performance. Again, given the levels of money and business exposure involved, it would be reasonable to expect a thoroughly competent and professional approach to system development. So let's take a quick look at one of the great global institutions at the heart of UK commercial transactions – the London stock exchange. There was a growing need for change and modernisation to meet the global competitive pressures. The system under review was TAURUS and it was going to revolutionise the way share transactions could be handled.

TAURUS

Before TAURUS (Transfer and Automated Registration of Uncertificated Stock), 'the City' did not have a particularly enviable reputation in investing in new technology. Caution and indecisiveness were more of the traditional trademark. One report, from an independent research organisation, established that a large number of computerised settlement systems were either ineffective or cancelled due to high cost overruns [25]. In a survey published in 1996, over 30% of users did not measure delivered 'value' of financial systems while over 50% did not carry out any form of benchmarking [26]. Overall, there seemed to be little mutual understanding of how to get IT applications into financial services. But all that was going to be drastically modified.

> The first major change to Stock Exchange transactions had already occurred in 1986 with the 'Big Bang' which started up the process of automated share dealing. The next stage would logically be the introduction of 'paperless' dealing as proposed by TAURUS. But this would ultimately lead to a considerable loss of jobs in the City and the parties concerned were both influential and disinclined to roll over

just to please some IT planners. In an effort to ensure that every voice in the land was heard, the Bank of England appointed a committee (the SISCOT committee – Securities Industry Steering Committee on TAURUS) to resolve issues and provide compromise solutions to outstanding problems as and when they arose. (Managing IT projects by committee is generally known as the 'kiss of death' approach, but perhaps this would be the exception.) A further number of local-interest groups formed various audit and monitor bodies – still without any central leadership or direction. Yet others formed political pressure groups. It started off in 1988 and rapidly became a parody of a development exercise. In full compliance with Murphy's Law, if something could go wrong, it did [27].

There were three fundamental expectations – each one alone sufficient to classify the project as a massive high-risk exercise:

a) simplification, where all the complex interactions and sign-offs needed to legalise a transaction should be dramatically reduced;
b) computerisation, to reduce the actual time to effect a transaction and to enable a much higher throughput of orders, and finally;
c) elimination of share certificates, replacing them with purely electronic records.

For all the problems of definition, announcements were made (either from the Stock Exchange, or from the SILCOT committee) extolling the system and the progress achieved. All development costs would be recovered within five years, and the costs of dealing in shares was going to be sharply reduced [28].

Completion date for the project proved to be a flexible parameter, moving easily from 1991 to 1993. Finally, two independent reports by consultants Andersen and Coopers & Lybrand suggested that a great deal more time and money would be needed to extract something from the mire. The major factors leading to this situation were:

- Lack of clear, documented objectives;
- Over-riding lack of leadership – technical and administrative;
- Poor decisions, particularly with regard to the selected database, led to unacceptable high costs of customisation;
- The culture of the members of the Stock Exchange was strongly traditional and was not ready for disciplined centralised technically-based operations.

The project was formally killed in early March, 1993 with a loss (depending on source) of between £100 million to £400 million.

Worse still was the loss of professional reputation of the London Stock Exchange round the world [29].

Over and above a strong application of Rule 1, one further output can be extracted from this project:

Rule 6   Lack of feasible, well-defined, and well-understood objectives will guarantee failure. It will either happen early or later on, but it will assuredly happen.

Medical systems

Medical procedures, processes, organisations, and systems should be in a class of their own because people's health and lives are at risk and, ultimately, errors can be fatal. For all that, systems for medical applications seem to show no particular superiority or dramatically better quality control than systems in general.

The London Ambulance Service (LAS)

In private industry, leaders and senior management can sometimes be fairly slow on the uptake, but they only tend to make the same mistake once. Learning may be hesitant, but it does exist. Not so with this one. This became a well known UK disaster project, the LAS, where people died as a direct result of an inadequate development program. OK, not nice but it happens. This was then properly followed up with an inquiry whose report was duly published, severely criticising the administration, its objectives and project implementation processes. The report concluded with a number of appropriate recommendations. So far so reasonable, but two years passed by and *it all happened again*. Unbelievably, someone died again, and for largely the same reasons.

The London Ambulance Service had started up in the 1930s and, after suitable expansion, was absorbed into the National Health Service in the 1970s. Using a form of 'message slips', i.e. literally written messages on pieces of paper, the incoming call is monitored and the message slip passed on to a suitable 'dispatcher' who will call up an available ambulance to handle the emergency. In the 1980s, automation was seen to be the way forward and, in 1987, the first contract was agreed to provide a limited upgrade to the dispatch operation. In 1990, following inevitable specification changes and some adverse test results, the entire project was cancelled. By early 1991, a wholly new state-of-the-art project had been conceived where the dispatching of the ambulance would be fully automated. The new system had a challenging specification, there was less than a year to deliver the first modules and the price was shaved to the bone. Guesses, anyone?

> By early February 1991, the new specification had been completed and the system planned to be operational the following January in 1992. By the end of March 1992, some tests of the first two phases of the system had been carried out and the units found to be inoperative (i.e. the system crashed). Some of the users and their union representatives blamed the system for degrading the overall ambulance performance leading to patient deaths. On the other hand, the Service itself was more inclined to blame human error in handling the new system. Whatever the cause, a number of doctors related stories of unacceptable delays (anything from one to five hours) and recorded messages being the only form of communication while the patient remained in desperate need of medical assistance [30, 31].
>
> Development continued through 1992 under reasonably ineffectual management until the first full installation and application of the system on the 26th October 1992. It was to prove an instant disaster and the decision to remove it was taken about 36 hours later at 2 p.m. on the 27th. The report of the subsequent public inquiry was published in February, 1993 and outlined some major structural criticisms which included:
>
> - The full system software was not complete, not tuned, and certainly not tested by the 26th October;
> - The hardware had not been tested for high traffic conditions;
> - There were no contingency plans or fallback options;
> - The staff had no confidence in the system and lacked training;
> - The system required near perfect inputs and these were not forthcoming due to high operator stress or lack of training.
>
> The overall result was that the system, as such, ground to a halt; the incoming demand totally exceeded the capability of the dispatchers to handle it; and the ambulance time-to-arrival moved up to the hours level. A number of recommendations were also given in the report in order to avoid any repetition of these unacceptable delays [32].

How did the management handle the situation? Well, by the following day – Wednesday 27th October – they claimed that there was not much of a problem and no-one had been seriously affected by the last few days. (Numbers seemed to have varied but the deaths of patients variously attributed to the non-working system appeared to be in the range of 20 to 40.) They then went on to claim that an excessive number of calls were made on the days in question (not so) and that the ambulance crews deliberately damaged the system (ditto). Regardless, the dispatchers went back to a semi-automatic approach until the next crisis on November 4th when the system again slowed to a halt and could not be rebooted. The reason was eventually found in a small untested software module, but the damage had been done. The LAS went back to full manual written operation and no further action was undertaken to match the recommendations of the report [33].

And that was the end of that particular crisis for the LAS. Until June 20th 1994 when 11 year old Nasima Begum desperately needed an ambulance. She was only minutes away from her hospital but her condition was not good. The ambulance service was repeatedly called and eventually arrived about one hour later. Nasima could, perhaps, have been saved if she had been treated in time, but treatment was delayed. She died a few hours later in hospital. After her death had caused a public outrage, a new plan for the LAS was finally instituted (see Chapter 9). It may be worth stressing that bad system design is not always a shared joke relating to poor management driving fantasy projects. Sometimes innocent people die.

America

Inadequate system design is not the sole prerogative of the UK. The conditions for poor development projects are sensibly universal and will be found in every commercial centre across the globe. In particular, there are lots of commercial centres in the USA and lots of examples of failed projects available [34]. Once again, all that is possible here is a brief overview of a few such projects to show how they conform to the general pattern.

Denver International Airport baggage handler

Through the late 1970s and 1980s, opinions hardened in Denver over the need to replace the existing airport with a brand new site that would do all the things that new airports are supposed to do. The 'decision to build' became political fact in 1989 when a referendum in favour was passed by 62% of the voters. The original plan called for completion by the Autumn of 1993 for an estimated cost of $2 billion. A significant part of the funding was to come from the sale of local bonds for which repayments were to begin 1ˢᵗ January 1994. (This restriction was to place enormous pressure on the development authority to finish the overall plan by this date, at the latest.)

In any airport one of the key interfaces between the commercial airline and the customer is the baggage handler – the ability to process the travelling baggage effortlessly and without error. For DIA, the new airport, it was felt that a state-of-the-art automated handler with high speed performance was required. A $200 million contract was awarded to develop one of the largest and most sophisticated baggage systems in the world (*yes, it does sound familiar*). But from the outset, time-to-complete was always going to be a bit of a problem. The Government Accounting Office report dated 14ᵗʰ October 1994 was still complaining about the non-operation of the baggage system. This system had managed, single-handedly, to keep the entire airport inoperative to the time of writing the report. Recall that the airport should have been open a year earlier and repayment of local bonds had started at the beginning of 1994. The system had done virtually everything to the luggage except deliver it to the wanted destination. It failed repeated tests with remarkable ease. The previously unacceptable conventional handler was eventually built as a fall-back solution, but it was still too slow for the airlines and it was never clear who was going to fund the additional outlay [34].

The basic problem became more understandable when the scheduling factor was examined. In the first instance, each airline was expected to provide its own baggage handler and United Airlines duly signed a contract with BAE – a major supplier of such equipment – in December 1991. Some time later the project management realised that a single standardised airport system was desirable, and requested bids from suppliers. BAE chose *not* to apply on the general grounds that the bid asked for 'too much too soon'. The City of Denver administration then rejected all the actual bids sent in and approached

BAE to take the contract. This was then awarded in April 1992 which left 18 months to design, develop, test, document, install and train staff on this large, complex, state-of-the-art system. And there were other problems:

- A Byzantine management structure had grown up around the overall project which meant that any negotiation for performance clarification, waivers, rights, space or airport access would be a time-consuming and frustrating exercise;
- Changes in senior personnel halfway through a time-pressed project tend to be difficult. One month after the baggage contract had been signed, the head of the DIA project resigned. The following October, the Chief Airport Engineer died. His replacement had a very different style;
- Throughout 1992 airlines started to move the goalposts, requesting changes to the basic operational specifications.

And so on. From here on, relations between the main management and BAE slid inexorably into conflict, with each side blaming the other. And there was never a hope in hell of reaching the original schedule [36].

Why go on? By now, it should be obvious that this complex, software-driven system was going to be a disaster without any reference to the software – it was all about people, decision interfaces, management cultures, understandings and perceptions and, perhaps, an (in)ability to relate to technical problems of disciplines other than your own. The two main bodies involved, the City of Denver project administration and BAE, always had two different agendas, time-scales, objectives, and languages. For the record, the airport opened commercially in February 1995. It was about two years late for a total outlay of roughly $5 billion and there was no single integrated baggage system on site.

California Department of Motor Vehicles

The DMV system development in the early 1990s was an expensive fiasco but it was not the first. A decade earlier, New Jersey DMV undertook a major new record-processing system implementation with Price Waterhouse as the development partner. All in all, it was not successful and the whole thing crashed horribly in 1985 having closed down the previous viable system. In computer terms, the California experience was a generation later, since the major development took place in the early 1990s. It had a different partner, Ernst & Young, and cost a great deal more, about $50 million, but the end result was pretty much the same. Judging by the events, one can only suppose some sort of collective hysteria took over an entire State organisation.

1987   The new proposal was put forward to enable car and driver data to be effectively processed. The system would cost about $30 million based on established IBM DB2 database technology. However, this approach was soon rejected and for the purposes of testing competitive tenders, simplified tests were proposed for a performance that was to be *half* the speed of the existing obsolete system.

1988   The Office of Information Technology (a somewhat ineffectual audit body whose job was to prevent wastage) agreed to allow DMV to build a working model for the purposes of evaluation only. Whatever the constraints, DMV went ahead with the main project.

1989   Ernst & Young were commissioned to propose a CASE (Computer Aided Software Engineering) tool for development purposes.

1990   Ernst & Young were unable to propose a suitable CASE tool, but DMV went on to select one on their own.

1991   DMV finally admitted that the selected CASE tool was not suitable for the intended purpose. By now budgets were getting stretched so contract labour was transferred to the developer, Tandem, so they could continue to be used and paid.

1992   DMV paid Tandem $46,000 for the wage bill for the contractors, but falsely declared this amount to be for software purchases.

1993   New proposals from Tandem (now in partnership with EDS) suggested that the total bill should rise to about $180 million to fully complete the development program. At this point, the State of California very reasonably stepped in and cancelled the entire project [37].

It is instructive how all the checks and balances built in to the State organisation were totally ineffective in controlling a runaway development program. There was the Office of Information Technology, a state watchdog which was strangely silent when all the rules were being broken. In addition, the Department of General Services, which existed to monitor contracting activities, allowed single-source contracts to be raised in the absence of any competitive bidding. The structures were in place, they just did not work [38].

NASA

Let me make my position clear: I am very much in favour of NASA (National Aeronautics and Space Administration). For decades, NASA was my role model for how professional engineering should be done. It was responsible for one of the two great engineering feats of this century – the first was the Apollo program in the 1960s for landing men on the moon while the other was the Manhattan Project at Los Alamos in the early 1940s. It is interesting how both of them broke the mould. After all that has been said in this chapter, note how both of them were complex, high risk, state-of-the-art technical projects, huge in extent and manpower, with monumental management structures, coupled to very long delivery schedules. And still they worked. So the next time you are up at 3 in the morning facing project disaster, keep these particular programs in mind – it *is* possible to get it right.

But times move on. There is a huge distance from the triumph of the Apollo 13 failure-to-success mission in 1970 to the cold agony of the Challenger shuttle as it blew apart in 1986 because the NASA Budget and PR departments appeared to be calling the shots rather than the Engineering and Quality functions.

> The latest thing is the space station. It all started back in 1984 when President Reagan announced his plan to build a permanent space station. It would take about 10 years to be launched. In 1988 it had reached the development stage and was given the name 'Freedom'. By 1990, the project was in serious financial trouble and from then on, change was order of the day and with every change from Congress (ostensibly to reduce the budget) came redesign which immediately increased the launch delay – and added to the budget. But the bottom line was that a lot of money had been squandered for not very much in return. For political (i.e. funding) reasons, a number of different sites had been selected for parts of the work and this approach was ultimately to prove an expensive exercise. Some of the proposed station components were 'make-work' or over-complicated and had to be reduced or eliminated. NASA, itself, was top-heavy

with bureaucracy and this slowed all decisions down to a crawl. Politicos ruled with a heavy hand.

By 1993 a much smaller station had evolved, Russia had became a partner in the grand design and the name was changed to 'Alpha'. But this all caused yet more losses as some parts could be adapted to the new product, and some parts could not. A lot of the developed sub-assemblies had to be jettisoned. The amount of money wasted over the 5 years of work has been variously estimated at about 50% of the total, i.e. in excess of $5 billion [39].

Even today, the management still suffers from major difficulties, and the balance of engineering quality and security against budgetry pressure remains a serious ongoing problem. Keep in mind that the current expenditure is planned to be about $13 billion *per annum*. By anybody's standards, that is a lot of room for potential waste. More worrying is the audit in the year 1999 that seems to highlight the same problems that were being identified in the year 1998. If these issues are not being addressed year on year, then the end result will almost certainly be an absence of good engineering – along with all that that entails [40].

Overview to Part 1

This section of the book has sought to establish, beyond any doubt, that a genuine problem exists, that it is both generic and global, and that the continued lack of any serious solution will prove to be a very expensive option in the future.

The problem under review is related to the development of new software systems for use in commercial applications. This is a universally popular undertaking but the majority of such development programs continue to fail. That is to say – they do not meet the original objectives in terms of timely delivery, meeting defined cost estimates or performing in line with the original technical specifications. What is particularly disturbing is that the picture appears largely unchanged over time. The surveys in Chapter 2 show the figures over the last decade from a number of different sources, and these provide a roughly constant success rate of about 15%. And this figure drops dramatically lower for large projects.

The last part, Chapter 3, looked at some actual case histories. The emphasis is not related to technical difficulties (although these are not unknown), but concentrates on the patterns of poor or indifferent management structures. Keep in mind that these studies were just a restricted selection of a far larger parent population of failed/failing projects, but the general conclusion would not have been altered if more examples had been given. Consider again the rules developed on the basis of these case histories given in simplified form in Table 3.1 below: they all relate to the human or social aspects of a project. Now go and look at some of the development exercises carried out in your own organisation – any common areas or points of contact?

Unfortunately, this has all been something of a prelude. These rules are important, but the real challenge requires a still more focused approach. It should be clear that the constraints outlined in Table 3.1 need to be fully addressed before any professionally planned project can be started up. But they are not enough in themselves. Assume all the rules, with the exception of Rule 5, have been followed. The projects have responsible leadership, technical competence, limited aims, defined objectives, and so on. There remains a very strong probability that the projects will continue to fail.

Table 3.1   The development project rule-book

Rule 1	If there is no accountable project leader, there is no project
Rule 2	If the funding is from a third party, budget is unimportant
Rule 3	If the project is 'huge' or 'complex', it cannot be managed
Rule 4	If the user does not want the system, do not develop it
Rule 5	If the original schedule is long, it will get longer (much longer)
Rule 6	If the objectives are poorly defined, the project will fail

Rule 5 is the real killer and the whole of Part 2 will be given over to looking at the conditions of long-interval projects to show that failure is virtually inevitable under these circumstances. Only after this has been made crystal clear can we begin to look at the solutions and work-arounds given in

Part 3. And, at the same time, look at how to handle all the other problem areas, once Rule 5 has been overcome.

References

1 Hall P, Great Planning Disasters, Penguin Books, 1981, p.170
2 Herbert S, Things are not looking up at the library, The Daily Telegraph, 4.11.94, p. 22
3 Blackhurst C, British Library 'will be 10 years overdue', The Independent, 27.11.95, p.
4 Report by the Comptroller and Auditor General, Progress in Completing the New British Library, HC 362 1995/96, 15.5.96
5 Bar-Hillel M, Reading between the lines, it's a disaster, The Evening Standard, 13.10.97, p.14
6 Hewitt V, MPs sound alarm on project's £1.2 bn bill, Computing, 1.12.88. p.1
7 Collins T, DSS system costs rise as staff snub Moore, Computing Weekly, 6.7.89, p.1
8 MP slates DSS systems failure, Computing, 20.6.91, p.9
9 Kelsey T, £2.6 bn DSS computer 'failure', The Independent, 9.9.94, p.1
10 Griffiths C and Willcocks L, Are major information technology projects worth the risk?, p.9, (see under Documents)
11 Collins T, £2.6 bn DSS system fails to hit targets, Computer Weekly, 28.3.96, p.1
12 Collins T and Bicknell D, Crash, p.128, (see under Bibliography)
13 Kelsey T, Flawed DSS computer system could cost £50m, The Independent, 8.7.94, p.1
14 Moules J, DSS sues ICL over failed benefit analysis software, Computing, 25.5.95, p.3
15 Walker P, 'No blame' in ICL Assist dispute, Computing, 19.6.97, p.6
16 Collins T, DSS setback stings Andersen for £25m, Computer Weekly, 2.5.96, p.1
17 Report by the Comptroller and Auditor General, The Contract to Develop and Operate the Replacement National Insurance Recording System, HC Session 1997-98, 29.5.98
18 ITSA denies Nirs liability, Computing, 29.4.99, p.2
19 Nissé J, Andersen criticised over computer chaos, The London Times, 10.7.99, p.23
20 Holmes D, MoD rejects Chots flak, Datalink, 9.5.88, p.6
21 Read M, MoD office project hits trouble as BT pulls out, Computing, 7.2.91, p.1
22 Evans J, MoD's IT gaffes prompt rap from watchdog MPs, Computing, 27.2.92, p.4
23 Collins T, MoD plans 'out-of-date' £14 m upgrade to Chots, Computer Weekly, 21.9.95, p.1
24 MoD confirms NT in ailing Chots project, Computing, 5.9.96, p.3
25 Fagan M, Brokers 'wasted £100m on systems', The Independent, 14.7.92, p.23
26 Bicknell D, City IT costs out of control, says survey, Computer Weekly, 4.1.96, p.3
27 Griffiths C and Willcocks L, Are major information technology projects worth the risk? p.16, (see under Documents)
28 International Stock Exchange: TAURUS Project, website : www.scit.wlv.ac.uk. ~cm1995/cbr/cases/case02/nine.htm
29 The Spectacular Collapse of the London Stock Exchange Project, MBA 832 Mini Case Studies, www.commerce.usask.ca/faculty/links/TEACHING/MBA832/London.htm
30 Hayward D, London Ambulance places dispatch system on sick list, Computing, 2.4.92, p.2

31 Jones J, Ambulance delays are blamed on staff errors, The Independent, 20.4.92, p.5

32 Randell B, London Ambulance Service Inquiry Report, *The Risks Digest*, Vol. 14, Issue 48, 7.4.93, p.2

33 Charette R, No One Could Have Done Better, *American Programmer*, July 1995, p.21

34 Glass R, Software Runaways, (see under *Bibliography*)

35 New Denver Airport : Impact of the Delayed Baggage System, Briefing Report, 10/14/94. GAO/RCED-95-35BR

36 Glass R, Software Runaways, p.35, (see under *Bibliography*)

37 Collins T and Bicknell D, Crash, p.221, (see under *Bibliography*)

38 US auditor counts cost of transport unit fiasco. US Bureau, *Computer Weekly*, 1.9.94, p.3

39 Carey J, 2002, A Space Odyssey – or just a Pork Pie in the Sky, *Business Week*, 15.8.94, p.47

40 National Aeronautics and Space Administration – 1999 Report, Inspector General: www.freedom.gov/results/ig99/nasa.asp

No light, but rather darkness visible,
Serv'd only to discover sights of woe,
Regions of sorrow, doleful shades, where peace
And rest can never dwell, hope never come
That come to all; but torture without end
Still urges

Paradise Lost, Book 1, Milton

Chapter 4   Analysis

Introduction to Part 2

Part 1 set out to establish that most system development exercises were pretty much doomed not to meet their original objectives.

The pattern is so consistent and the probability of success so low that there will have to be yet another hard look at the underlying reasons why success is so elusive. Note the one over-riding fact that we will come back to again and again: systems are continuing to fail up to the present moment – much as they have since the 1950s. Once this status is accepted as valid (and this is what Chapters 2 and 3 were all about), then it follows that all the investigations, models, studies, proposals, strategies, recommendations and reports carried out to date on development methods must be considered as suspect. Not necessarily wrong – but still suspect.

By comparison look at some of the new techniques pioneered in medicine, such as the various image scanners, key-hole surgery, and IVF. In each case, the first results were poor and, within a matter of years, reliable, consistent methods were developed. Space engineering has moved from the tentative to the confident. The progress made in the performance and reliability of computer hardware has been bordering on the fantastic – and offered to the consumer at ever falling prices into the bargain. It is time to find reasons why software development, almost alone, has pursued its chosen Cinderella role so consistently over the last few decades.

The last chapter of this section will consider the human side of strategic system development, but first, in the next three chapters, we will review the problems and challenges that exist right up at the front end of the exercise. These are the crucial processes and mechanisms which establish the net performance, cost and timescales of a new system project and start it on its way. In many ways, a new system start-up can be likened to a bridge that connects the past operations of the organisation to the future, more effective, administrative processes. The bridge is supported by three main development pillars as shown in Figure 4.1. If any one of these supports is weakened or cannot take the strain, then clearly the bridge structure itself will be in serious danger.

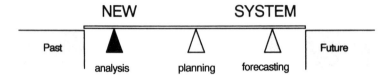

Figure 4.1   The underpinning of new systems

One last point. Before we begin to look at the first topic, there is a key characteristic of the development process that is worth previewing.

We can start with a quick look at 'maintenance', the last of the activities in the development life cycle [1]. The cost of carrying this out has been variously estimated to be in excess of 50% of the total development cost [2,3,4]. In other words, maintenance can be expected to cost more than all other development activities put together. A major part of this figure is associated with the cost-to-repair, i.e. the cost of sorting out the system bugs, defects and malfunctions discovered during operations after delivery to the client.

Figure 4.2 gives a breakdown view of the relative maintenance costs of repairing errors generated in the different sectors of the life cycle [5]. Each division of the chart is equivalent to multiplying the overall cost by about 3. Thus it will be 9 times more costly to go back to the coding level to cure some bug as it would be to have to go back to the installation level - which is two levels further down the development path.

It is arguable what the exact ratio ought to be for every development phase. However, what should be self-evident is that a bug in the analysis phase only discovered after delivery to the client is going to be the most expensive sort of error to correct. Every part of the design cycle will need to be repeated in order to correct the error. Summarising briefly, mistakes in analysis will ultimately prove very costly to the project.

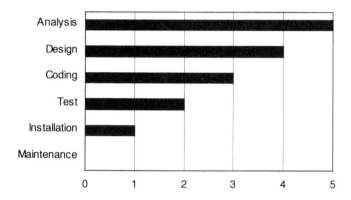

Figure 4.2   The log of the cost ratio for system repair

With all that in mind, we are finally ready to take a look at the first key development support. And let's make sure that we are all talking about the same thing:

Analysis   Activities undertaken to establish the nature and operation of the existing software system application, and possibly a review of any new proposed enhancements. These may include related feasibility and organisational studies.

The way to tackle it will be to use a two-pass approach – the first time to identify the key objectives, and the second time to establish the potential fault modes in operation. Note that this is a slightly different structural breakdown from the conventional model. It is a merging of what are usually two separate processes: the Feasibility study and the Analysis phase. But they both provide essentially the same output – the breakdown of all the elements that make up the old system. One provides it after a short period of review, while the other provides a more in-depth investigation of the same material as a basis for new design.

Analysis goals

At the outset, it will be prudent to define the scope of the exercise. In a simplified form this will include the following activities:

❑ Capture;

❑ Justification;

❑ Capability;

❑ Scope;

❑ Definition.

Capture

In any evolutionary framework, to create the new you have to understand the old. In the software development context, there will need to be a comprehensive understanding of all aspects of the existing system as it is currently applied within the organisation. This knowledge is held by the hands-on users who are the only ones who really know how the system operates on a day to day basis. The mechanics of reaching out to the user group will need to be taken from one or more of the following techniques.

Interviews   This can be based on a structured or more informal set of conversations taking place between an end-user and one interviewer. Alternatively, it could be a group of end-users and interviewers simply talking round a table.

Forms   This approach can be helpful if there are a number of multi-site users involved in applying the same system, and the form writer has a clear idea of exactly what is needed. A structured questionnaire can be a useful way of interfacing with a larger group of users.

Role-play   This can be a productive tool where you are evaluating the co-operative interaction of a team of operators. It is often easier to act out a particular set of operations than to describe it formally on paper. It has the added advantage of involving more than one user in commenting on the same process.

Pilot   This is a form of prototyping where a simple (non-working) model of the process under review can be put up on the screen for discussion and review by the users. For example, a screen indicating a list of choices may carry the wrong options, be in the wrong format, or even not be in the right company colours.

Justification

Is there a case to be made for undertaking all this work? Clear answers will have to be provided for the following questions.

Strategy   Will the new system interact effectively with the existing systems and procedures of the organisation? Will it fit into the planned strategic objectives?

Company   Are the management, end-users and other parties likely to accept the new proposed system. Will there be significant training costs?

Technology   How dramatically different is the new proposal? Is it just an upgrade from the previous system, a major new innovation, or a total revolution?

P. and L.   What are the first estimates for the cost of the system work and how will this cost be recovered by the use of the system? And is there an estimate for how many years after installation it will take to break even?

Capability

If the previous section asks 'do we want it?' then this section poses the question 'in any case, can we do it?'

Schedule   Is the proposed development time realistic for all the activities involved – including, say, documentation writing and approval and workforce training? Is the time scale for the system introduction acceptable in terms of corporate need?

Skills   Are the necessary technical and management capabilities currently available in the organisation? Are the required hardware platforms and software development tools available and already in use?

Funding   Is there a budget available for some sensible estimated cost of development? Is there an overspend capability?

Scope

Finally, there is the listing of identified decisions and options that have either been addressed in the feasibility study, or will need to be addressed as part of the first steps in the analysis. A simplified set of the basic decisions relating to the development framework could include:

❑ Design methodology   Unified set of development processes

❑ Hardware platform   Required processor and periphals

❑ Database structure   RDBMS or OO format

❑ Development tools   e.g. CASE tool or OO environment

❑ Network configuration   Client Server structure

❑ Web elements   Internet and web site involvement

❑ Security, reliability   Firewall, encryption, backup, etc.

❑ User support   Training, help desk, call centre, etc.

This is not a complete list, but each one of these is a major strategic decision area in its own right.

Definition

This is the eventual formulation of the new proposed system and comprises three activities following on sequentially from one another :

Translation All the information relating to the existing system can now be transcribed into a standard format using appropriate diagramming tools (such as the Entity Relationship Diagrams).

Projection Starting from these diagrams representing the existing system, design modifications can be introduced to evaluate possible new system approaches.

Distribution Reports and specifications outlining the new proposals will be sent to all interested parties for comment, and, ultimately, acceptance.

Summary

The above few pages more or less wrap up the feasibility and analysis target activities as recognised in most books today. At this point, all is sweetness and light. It starts with an examination of the old existing methods and seems to move smoothly and effectively to the proposals for a new enhanced system. But, in reality, it turns out there are still some problems outstanding. Some relatively serious problems...

Fault modes in analysis

The analytical phase is the most difficult to implement and the most costly to repair. Under these circumstances, Murphy's Law naturally ensures that major problems will arise. This section will set out to investigate such problems and identify the key difficulties.

Developer - client interface

Over a period of some years there will be intensive and continuing contact between the developers and the client - both at the managerial and end-user level. For the project to have any real chance of success, this contact must be based on mutual trust and respect – and this will be critically established over the first few meetings.

Interviewing the users

The essence of this activity is that someone asks the user some questions and it is assumed that the answers returned will be truthful and complete. This assumption should, at minimum, be open to review.

Consider a particular group of workers belonging to the finance department of an organisation. One day, a stranger is introduced to them by their Personnel or HR department. This stranger talks well, is smartly dressed and all he or she wants is to analyse their activities. He isn't offering them more money or more holidays, he is just looking for a full and accurate description of their staff interaction and how they handle specific work-related tasks. In effect, all that is intended is ultimately to increase their productivity by designing and installing a new IT management system. At the same time their overall numbers will probably be reduced substantially as a means of justifying and paying for the new system. That, at least, is the message from the office rumour-mills.

A moment's reflection will show that this is just a modern version of the time-and-motion studies carried out in the heavy industries throughout the late 19th century and early 20th century. The workforce then would go to considerable lengths to ensure that the data collected by the engineer favoured their side of the argument. In the same way, today, if some altogether reasonable person with an electronic clipboard approaches, it may not be in the best possible interests of the workforce to co-operate with this individual. The probability is that this altogether reasonable person will be directly threatening their own livelihood within a short space of time [6]. In their place, what would you do?

All of which leaves open the vexed question of good relationships and the means of obtaining reliable information about the existing system. The developer still needs that information as a baseline and the users are still the best, if not the only, source. There are no easy generic answers and each case will have to be considered with some care. But it is still a bit of a problem.

The first meeting

The first date, the first job interview, the opening night and the pilot prototype are all the same. The parties concerned are nervous, they are mixing with strangers on unfamiliar territory, they cannot give of their best and there is tremendous uncertainty whether the 'thing', whatever it is, is ever going to take off. The only plus in these situations is that the next time round it is going to be a whole lot easier as familiarity brings a rise in self-confidence and encourages a closer working relationship.

Which is precisely the problem for software feasibility and analysis studies. Every time is nearly always the first time, and every time carries the same stressful disadvantages outlined above. This is because, unlike more conventional exercises such as bridge building or plane design, every new project is virtually unique in terms of applying the latest technology, hardware, and software strategies. There has always been a high personnel turnover in software development, and the end-users and development staff will usually have changed considerably from, say, three years ago. In effect, there is no 'old-boy' network to call up. Or, more likely, a completely new development partner has been selected. The external market may have changed out of all recognition – Russia is in, Scotland has gone independent, taxes are up and the client has just merged with a competitor. To add to the problems, the experience gained on the last project is probably either inappropriate or obsolete – or both. Check this one out in your own organisation – what was the planned information technology objectives four or five years ago? Were you looking then at the typical year 2000 workload – investigating object oriented databases, designing data warehouse applications, using Java for your intranet web site {*Java? Intranet? Web site?*}. What percentage of your current development staff were designing systems in the same location three years ago? How different were your documentation strategies, methodologies, operating systems, quality targets and test procedures?

Recapping, virtually every analysis carried out for a significant new project will usually be characterised by the new design team tackling a highly innovative project - using platforms and techniques that were probably only developed over the last five years. All of which tends to make this activity a first-time non-repeatable learning-from-new event. Every time. As a result, it may well be overly optimistic to assume a low-error output or quality result from the analysis phase. Remember, no-one ever gets it right the first time round.

Interaction

At a more general level, clients and designers do not seem to form good working relationships. It is not clear why, but a survey of IT users by the National Computing Centre found a number of serious communication problems between the two. The IT professionals need to improve their selling and negotiating skills while the users do not recognise or understand the significance of the IT related activity [7]. This is backed up by some tragi-comic accounts given by business managers on just how appalling some IT project meetings have been [8]. This message is further underlined by another survey carried out in 1995 (*IT and corporate strategy - Towards a common goal*) which suggested that about 60% of business managers did not know what went on in the IT department [9]. Again, [9] goes on to discuss the profound communication barrier that seems to exist between the business managers and the associated IT managers. Predictably, each party complains about the attitudes and lack of co-operation of the other side. This important topic will be further discussed in Chapters 10 and 11.

Summary

This section opened by stressing the need for a good rapport between developers and their clients. Its overall importance does not seem to have been fully recognised to date and, in general terms, good results have not been achieved. Trust between the system-developers and the client end-users has never been high, familiarity with the changing technology remains poor, and the client management still seem to perceive development as a necessary evil and system people as fast-talking spenders. Under these circumstances, the corresponding impact on project success is unlikely to be a surprise. This will be further illustrated in Chapter 7 where the LITS case study shows an almost complete breakdown in the developer/client relationship and what happened to the project as a result.

Business goals

It would seem a reasonable and necessary objective that the technical deliverables and installed IT performance should match and assist the organisation's commercial goals. It may be reasonable, but, in seeking this match, two main problems arise:

Misdirected objectives

There is an increasing tendency to concentrate on meeting budget and schedule targets while forgetting the original intent, i.e. to design and install a new system to meet some cost-effective, competitive or strategic target. A recent study by KPMG found that, while 90% of companies surveyed said that their projects were successful (which, of itself, is somewhat at variance with the results of Chapter 2), only 25% of them had measured the business benefit. It seems that project success is not measured by any corresponding strategic advantage [10]. This view is backed up by another survey by Braxxon Technology where one third of all directors questioned admitted that IT was not delivering value for money and another third did not know since they could not measure the effectiveness. On another topic, more than a third of the directors suggested that their IT was only moderately successful in aligning with their business objectives [11].

Inadequate monitors

A repeated theme, with regard to meeting strategic targets, is that there are no tools to measure the commercial benefit, if any, of an IT implementation. This is borne out by the survey *The IT Impact Survey* carried out in 1997 which specifically highlighted this problem. Even when it is thought that some strategic or competitive benefit has been obtained, there is still no means of quantifying this benefit [12]. This is an critical parameter and will be discussed more extensively in Chapter 6.

Summary

This may not be considered a crucial topic, but the aligning, or misaligning, of system projects with the corporate strategic aims will have a significant impact on the eventual success they achieve. However, if any assumed system success cannot be measured or quantified then the perceived value of this success must remain seriously open to question.

Dream-ware

The totally dedicated fervour which some men and women bring to bear to achieve their goals has resulted in some fantastic tales of bravery and determination leading to eventual success. There have also been other cases – of tragic loss, abject failure and embarrassing banana skins. In the main, software project dream-ware seems to fall into the latter category, and it would be prudent to recognise the early warning symptoms.

It often starts with a senior manager or chief executive. And, sure enough, he or she has a dream: to be the first or the best or the most advanced. This actually happened to the FoxMeyer Drug company, a successful pharmaceutical firm located in Texas.

> It started in 1994 with a very ambitious multi-million dollar project for monitoring and controlling orders from the company warehouse. It was going to reduce handling costs, improve inventory control and provide the clients with strategically helpful information. (*Someone must have been reading about 'competitive advantage'*.) It was advanced technology, it was extending the boundary, and it was always going to be reasonably expensive. But confidence was high – it is said that FoxMeyer took the projected savings into account with its next round of bidding for contracts. The problem was that the daily transaction volumes were probably too high for the selected system implementation, business considerations brought forward the commercial operation date and the state-of-the-art system never worked properly anyway. An important client stopped trading – and therefore stopped ordering, the space-age warehouse fixtures were late, and ongoing errors in meeting orders caused further losses due

to unrecoverable costs. Inside two years, this one system development had taken the firm into bankruptcy [13, 14].

Another example of a software system touted to be the 'largest and most advanced' is the Swanick £350 million air traffic control centre in the UK. However large or advanced the system really is, the one thing beyond doubt is that it is late. It is currently more than three years behind schedule [15]. Again, many of the case studies given in Chapter 3 seem to have started life as the largest, or the most technologically challenging, etc., etc. The presence of superlatives in the marketing material does appear to provide an early warning signal of an impending disaster.

Another type of early warning is given by the sort of *folie de grandeur* sometimes shown by senior management. It is manifested by requesting the development of a software system application where the scheduled delivery dates and development budget have already been fixed to some arbitary level. This is exactly what happened in one large project in the US where a consortium of companies worked to develop a system. Again, this was to prove just a starting point as the project eventually sank at some later testing stage further down the line, but it was surely an ominous beginning [16].

User requirements

It is worth recalling that the first, and most important, function of analysis is to accurately capture the nature of the existing currently-used system. The second function is then to modify this system view such as to produce the basis for the next system design and implementation. Generating precise user requirements is obviously important for effective project definition and this is underlined by being the one area identified as critical by all the surveys evaluated in Chapter 2.

And it is virtually guaranteed to fail.

To get a better understanding of why this should be so, we can take a look into the two potential problem areas at the start of every new project: the client and the developer.

The client

Assume that you have never been to sea before, but wish to learn to sail. You are looking, perhaps, to purchase a 37 foot sea-going sailing vessel for regular use during the summer months. How do you go about selecting such a boat, which tends to be an expensive one-off outlay?

The answer usually given is that you cannot possibly know what sort of sailing will eventually interest you until you have developed your sailing skills. Equally, you cannot possibly know what features you will consider important in a boat until you have applied those skills. Under these circumstances, the solution is reasonably simple: do not buy a 37 foot boat. Instead, buy a cheap 16 foot boat and 'potter around' on an estuary for the next year. At the end of that time, you will know far better what type of large boat will match your requirements and will be able to specify the needed features precisely and cost-effectively.

In a similar way, an IT system client cannot possibly know what will be needed for the next generation administration tool. Having spent, say, a few years running the existing system, he or she will be well-versed in the current version and its application potential. However, projecting that knowledge upward into an advanced system using the latest IT strategies and products is just not going to happen overnight. He may well learn what he needs and what is on offer from the new technology, 6 to 12 months into the project, but never at the outset. This explains why 'project creep' tends to occur (the gradual modification and extension of the user requirements over a period of time which leads inevitably to increased rework schedules and costs) and why it is considered so necessary or irritating - depending on your viewpoint [17,18]. Various disciplines have been proposed to enable user requirements to be reliably generated [19], but we always return to the same criterion: at the start of a project, the user will not have enough experience or knowledge to define the scope of a wanted system. (There is a lot to be said for investing, if possible, in some low cost stop-gap version of a system equivalent to the 16 foot boat.)

The developer

On the other side, novelty is again the enemy. The development group has been assembled from available staff (or it could even be a potent mix of in-house development engineers, consultants, contractors and out-sourced facilities teams). The fundamental issue remains: how can the technical staff liaise with the users to provide advice and assistance on the system options available? In most instances, they will not understand the business that the user is in. That is normal. However, in addition they are now starting up this new, complex, largely unknown technology that will be applied to the project. It will need a high investment on their part to become proficient in, say, a year's time. But they are being asked to provide answers now.

Take, as an example, the development team being switched over from a relational to an OO (Object Oriented) data system project. This type of transition may or may not be desirable, but it is occurring reasonably frequently in the present climate. In this case, how much attention should one pay to the team's initial inputs on the test philosophy, strategy, environment, duration and actual test performance criteria? Clearly, not too much, as OO testing specifications can call for a lot of professionalism and OO development experience [20]. And much the same will apply to documentation structures, design methodologies, communication procedures, project milestone definitions, and authorisation sign-off standards. In effect, unless the design group is comfortable with the proposed technology, any functional specification that is written will be practically worthless - even with the support of the client users.

Evolving a development team up to a new technology is roughly equivalent to asking a world-class figure skater to join a top-grade ice-hockey team. It may eventually work well, but it going to take a lot of effort and a lot of time. And this may not always be available.

Summary

The start-up phase of a new system development carries some inherent problems which will tend to limit the accuracy of any parametric values that are obtained in this phase. These values will be crucial for later project activities. There are six key factors that will always radically affect project start-ups:

❏ There are no defined or standardised procedures for implementing the feasibility and analysis phases;

❏ With finite effort within a finite timespan, there can never be full capture of the existing system data. Neither the actual percentage missing nor its criticality can be determined at this point;

❏ There are no established test criteria that can validate any summaries or conclusions reached;

❏ Every start-up tends to be with new personnel, new technologies, and new working environments;

❏ There are, at best, only limited skills in the design team for soliciting information from the user, who, in any case, may not wish to co-operate;

❏ In a start-up system project, there is practically no way for the client to actually know what specific requirements he should demand nor for the developer to know how to meet those requirements.

References

1 Maintenance (see *Appendix 2*)
2 Parikh G, Techniques of Program and System Maintenance, QED Informational Sciences, 1988, p.13
3 Project costs: Maintenance takes a two-thirds slice, Computer Weekly, 21.3.1991, p.1
4 Peverett T, Managing the maintenance crisis, Informatics, August 1991, p.31
5 Data View: Cost of correcting software errors, Computer Weekly, 20.6.1991, p.1
6 Leung L, Prepare user specifications, Computing, 12.9.1996, p.36
7 Survey of IT users, NCC, 1994, p.14
8 Evans D, IT bosses: What we want from you, Computer Weekly, 4.7.1991, p.15
9 Boyle B, Why IT and business managers must talk, Computer Weekly, 29.6.1995, p.16
10 Kavanagh J, Blind leading the blind into IT fog, Interface, The London Times, 6.8.1997, p.10
11 Bicknell D, City IT costs out of control, says survey, Computer Weekly, 4.1.1996, p.3
12 Infomonitor, IT impact continues to defy precise measurement, Information Age, October 1997, p. 5
13 James G, IT fiascoes...and how to avoid them, Datamation, November 1997
14 Glass R, Software Runaways, p.104, (*see under Bibliography*)
15 Collins T, The curse of the optimistic project instigators, Computer Weekly, 19.3.1998, p.36
16 Zells L, Litigated Disaster: The anatomy of a major product failure, Application Development Trends, November 1994, p.43
17 Isham P, Promising the earth will only end in tears, Computer Weekly, 5.8.1993, p.18
18 Donnelly F, Plan for all seasons, Computing, 4.6.1992, p.32
19 Jirokta M and Goguen J (editors), Requirements Engineering: Social and Technical Issues, Academic Press, 1994
20 Webster B, Pitfalls of Object-Oriented Development, p.206, (*see under Bibliography*)

Chapter 5 Planning

Long term projects

For large system developments, planning has long been established as a significant part of the strategic imperative. It constitutes the second major support for new system projects – see Figure 5.1. Handbooks on project management, up to the present time, continue to explore the need for ever more complex and ever more detailed planning tools, but this chapter will set out to show just how dangerously ineffective system project planning can be in the real world.

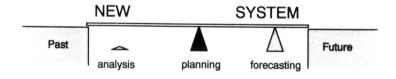

Figure 5.1 The underpinning of new systems

As a foretaste of the arguments and problem areas to be reviewed later, let's start with a quick look at the *Charles de Gaulle*, the new French aircraft carrier currently under construction and fitting out at Brest.

The 38,000 ton nuclear powered craft was first considered as a replacement in the early 80s; construction work was started in 1989; the carrier was launched in 1994; commissioning was planned for 1999; and the date for entering active service was intended to be 2001 – although this has currently been deferred to 2004. The current estimated cost is about £2 billion (and rising). First sea trials took place in January 1999 and this led to unresolved problems with the propulsion units – one of which caught fire. Two months later, the carrier was incarcerated in dry dock at Brest for an indeterminate period [1, 2].

Clearly this project could well be turning into the Gallic equivalent of the British National Library – wildly overpriced, grossly over-schedule, and frustratingly under-performing. Fine, but none of our concern, unless we happen to belong to the French military or French taxpayer class. However, now consider the main points about the hardware and software computer elements driving all those ship operations, communication networks and sophisticated weapon control systems.

❏ It is intended to be on active duty halfway through the first decade of the new millennium, say 2005.

❏ It must have been planned some time between 1982 and 1997, i.e. two years before intended active service. It seems reasonable to assume that the computer facilities were first seriously specified and designed about 1989 at the start of the work; and finally installed around launch time in 1994.

❏ Now consider the available PC technology of 1989 when these systems were likely to be specified. (This set of data was taken from suitable magazines of the period [3, 4].)

Hardware :	30386 Chip at 20 Mhz; 2 Mb Ram; 68 Mb Hard Disc; 5¼ inch floppy
O.S :	DOS v.3.3/Windows v2.03
Database :	DBase IV; Foxbase v2; Oracle v5.1

The bottom line is that none of this material would be suitable for installation in some mid-90s state-of-the-art performance systems. However much planning was undertaken, all the system components (whether mainframe, mini or PC hardware and software) are likely to have become completely obsolete and would need to be fully changed, re-specified, re-approved, re-documented, re-tested and re-installed. That would get it up to, say, 1997/8 standard. But for 2004/5, the whole lot will almost certainly need to be to be upgraded once again. (Shades of the CHOTS project from Chapter 3).

It may be stating the obvious, but the real problem with long-term planning is change.

The planning role

It is time to take a step back and define the area of interest. In the first place, we can cover the real expectations of project planning, looking at it from the more or less conventional corporate viewpoint.

Key objectives

Planning is carried out at the start of any project and is subsequently monitored for the duration of the ongoing program of work. It is concerned with defining, outlining and tracking all the major activities that will be carried out in order to develop and install a commercial system. There are two main areas of interest:

Requirements

Pretty much like all other activities carried out in the organisation, the initial planning work should be:

Competent	The project manager will need to have proven expertise in planning.
Pertinent	The work should be focused on the task in hand and, at the same time, should ensure that it will meet the long-term objectives of the organisation.
Comprehensive	Full coverage of all the needed activity.
Feasible	Practical within the bounds of available budget, development facilities and skills.

Control

Once the project has got under way, Program Management (PM) will continue to monitor the progress made. In the event that any deviations to the master plan should be detected, PM must be able to control events (or inform with all due speed those who do control events) such as to eliminate the impact of the source deviation and to maintain the planning objectives.

Justification

What is the point of planning? More precisely, what is the impact to the specific project or to the overall organisation if development planning is not carried out?

One classical view – mid-1980s – suggests that good planning is a pre-requisite for good results from a system project. It further suggests that time spent at the front end getting the planning program 'right' is time well spent, and that accurately predicted event dates or activity durations will materially help the project over the coming years. The picture emerges of a well-defined formal process establishing all the major milestones of the project right at the outset of the development exercise. Note that this forecast will occur perhaps years before any of the related activities will actually be undertaken [5].

Another approach is to analyse existing projects for signs of inadequate performance. In this context, projects in trouble, i.e. poorly planned programs, will be characterised by restricted goals, communications, controls and quality. In turn this will generally result in delivering the wrong product, containing poor workmanship and all for a heavily inflated price [6]. Structured planning clearly has some value.

Problem areas

The theory is well established. You want to develop a new system. Spend a few weeks identifying and listing all the things that have to be applied or developed. Call the resulting list 'User Requirements'. Now attach a sensible delivery date to every item in the list. Call this new document 'Program Schedule'. Finally, during the following phases of the development life cycle, keep the design team delivering products defined in the user requirements in line with the dates agreed in the program schedule. Stand back and wait for the well-deserved end-of-year bonus.

But it does not always work that way.

Good user requirements are a vital part of the development process. However, the identification, documentation and delivery of accurate requirements will heavily depend on both the user and the developer understanding a number of crucial aspects of the business:

❑ The ongoing changing nature of the applied technology, the external market, and the development environment;

❑ The core objectives of the commercial organisation; and

❑ The way in which IT can provide a strategic advantage in meeting those core objectives.

Judging by results up to the present, these issues continue to be largely ignored at the time of any new project start-up [7, 8].

Change and its impact

Let's go back to fundamentals. This part of the chapter will look at the different forms of change which can seriously threaten existing planning goals. The basic factors are outlined in Figure 5.2 and these can individually and collectively degrade the planning targets – sometimes to the point of project extinction. The impact of these various factors will be dependent on the amplitude, the frequency and the 'attack rate' or speed with which the change is introduced to the development program. These issues will be addressed later in the section.

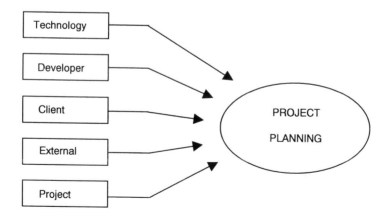

Figure 5.2   The threat of change to project planning

Technology

Consistently, over the last thirty years, improvements in scientific understanding, engineering capabilities and manufacturing processes have been the collective dynamo powering the next generation of ever-improved technical products. Nevertheless, when the component replacement cycle is faster than the commercial product development period, serious planning problems occur. The classic example was the need to replace all the existing electric wiring in the new British National Library because its useable life was already exceeded *before the building had even been opened to the public.* Perhaps a more typical example would be the CHOTS project (see Chapter 3) where there was a consistent need to change the technology every few years to keep up with the expectations of the client – moving the user interface from DOS to Windows for example. Whenever a new processor chip, or printer, or modem, say, dramatically improves the existing performance and becomes the new 'standard' for the project component, then the project schedule will be materially affected, and always for the worse. Extra development cycles will be needed in the product plans to accommodate the new required enhancements and upgrades. (As, perhaps, for the systems on a new aircraft carrier under long-term development.)

This whole problem of changing technology can be encapsulated with the old maxim from Edward Young (slightly modified):

Innovation is the thief of time.

Developer

The main problem here is the changing nature of the team working on the project. Over any given period of time, programmers, system analysts, test engineers, managers, along with all the other critical participants, have the habit of leaving the company or the country; or having heart attacks or nervous breakdowns. Or having their children do it for them. Or they lose/gain (misplace?) their partner or pet. Or members of their immediate family. Or the Volvo.

What is clear is that any of the above events will tend to be a distraction to the project-related human resource and will significantly reduce the quality of the work output. What is more, Murphy's law ensures that the timing will either be random and completely unforeseeable, or it will occur at the worst possible moment. So plan for it to happen and let a little contingency burst into your life [9].

In addition, note that any replacement staff imported to overcome the above problems will frequently:

a) Not get on with the original team/boss/secretary/clients;

b) Have a completely different set of priorities to the rest of the team;

c) Need time and tuition to understand the project objectives and how the organisation itself operates; and

d) Still be subject to all the problems listed in the first paragraph above.

Client

The client will often be the major culprit in this area:

Strategic drift

As the group objectives evolve and change over time, so the existing system priorities will be modified. If, for example, the company seeks an alliance with another organisation, the original need for the system undergoing development may be completely changed.

Requirement-creep

This was discussed in the last chapter. The client learns over time more about the possibilities of IT as an aid to meeting their existing administrative or commercial objectives. As this happens, so their original requirements will be modified to a more interactive, complex, and somewhat more challenging level.

Isolation

In an effort to reduce the need for change, the client is often kept away from the ongoing performance of the developing system until final handover. The subsequent reaction to the system that, the client contends, will not meet their needs, can often be explosive and litigious.

Crisis

From time to time, dramatic events may radically change the financial status of the client. When this happens, the budget may, for example, be halved, or the development team may suddenly find themselves with double or treble the workload. This is perhaps the one time when leading the workforce over the barricades is not going to help much. So relax.

External

Another problem area – the world outside will not go away. The development costs of the new system may be based on a certain tax situation. If that tax status changes after the next budget, the whole justification for the project may require a drastic re-appraisal. Similarly, the formal entry/non-entry of the UK into the European currency may change the entire objectives of a financial payment system. Or the change in the Sales tax in New York State may modify the feasibility of a proposed new hospital system. In terms of systems under current development, continued vigilance in monitoring current affairs is commended. It may help to avoid unpleasant surprises.

Project

The actual project, its objectives and goals, its standards and deliverables, the client and developer teams – it starts to take on a life of its own. For a few years, perhaps, it develops a culture, the 'crowd', a set of 'in' buzz-words, gossip and scandal sources – a true micro-world. And it is a world in evolution that continues to change over the life of the development, in turn affecting the overall progress of the project.

Management

Every time a new management structure or team is veneered onto the project sub-structure, the priorities and 'style' will be varied leading to a new learning curve for the rest of the staff.

Reviews

Usually a major project review is held perhaps twice a year. The result will inevitably lead to some limited changes in objectives and schedules (how else to justify the review?) which, in turn, will lead to a healthy re-work cycle to meet the new requirements.

Decisions

An ailing project orphan will possibly drag its tired feet from schedule update to schedule update for maybe a year (say, the user interface 'help screen' definition). Suddenly, it is agreed to make this a 'phase II' activity.

In this case, the available resources can now be re-allocated to existing jobs with corresponding changes to delivery targets. Conversely, it could have become a priority item, with a corresponding need for increased resources.

Hiccups

Every so often, a sudden shift in project operations occurs. This time round, it is decided that more money should be invested in setting up better 'review committees' or 'test facilities' or 'training manuals'. Conversely, it could equally be an overall 20% reduction in operating budget - say, all overtime to be stopped as of tomorrow. Usually one follows the other. Either way, the planning disruption can be expected to last a reasonable number of weeks.

Backlash

Any stable, contented community will tend to fight off changes that threaten the existing habits and customs of the group. The development of resistance to change over time is the unexpected surprise here and it may need a lot of repeated effort to move the project into some new direction [10].

Impact of change

The last few pages have addressed a number of possible mechanisms that could critically affect the progress of a software project. What has to be covered now are the knock-on effects that these mechanisms will cause to the project. The principal factors are:

Non-linearity

Consider a car on the road that is about to stop. A light pressure on the brake pedal will cause the car to slow down. More pressure will cause the braking to be more effective. This is a standard linear response: double the input, double the effect. Now consider that the same process is occurring on ice. Once again, limited pressure will cause limited stopping. But more pressure on the pedal this time will cause the driver to lose control and the car to skid. A completely non-linear non-predictable response.

Most changes to a development program generate a similar non-linear output, that is – the effect tends to be out of all proportion to the input. In turn, this means that the risk associated with a particular change is hard to quantify. The loss of one senior programmer could potentially be irrelevant or, alternatively, put the entire project at risk.

Frequency

Most formally planned projects can handle one, maybe two, serious modifications. But, at some time or another, *all* the inputs discussed in this section will be bound to occur. If a project lasts, say, six years – it will never stop carrying out major upgrades and repairs for most of that time.

Attack rate

For most situations, the more suddenly the change mechanism appears – the greater the impact. If you knew for the last year, say, that the avionic computers would not fit in the allocated aircraft slot, then some contingency planning could have been undertaken. If the problem is only encountered at the system integration phase, it is much more than likely you would simply shut up shop and go home (see the cost factors in Figure 4.2 on page 55). This seems to have actually happened with one classic design of some radar equipment for the RAF Nimrod program which was cancelled when exactly this problem arose [11]. Do not ask what the British taxpayer paid for this exercise.

Now take a few moments out and look back over the main points of the last few pages. Because with these points we are finally in a position to analyse 'planning' in software development and to understand why it has such an appallingly poor track record with system development projects up to and including the present.

The system planning environment

Just a short interlude to set the scene. Remember, from the section 'The planning role' earlier in this chapter, there were two key activities that were needed to carry out a viable planning exercise. Without them, there could be no sensible likelihood of success :

❑ A comprehensive definition of the user requirements;

❑ Full control maintained over the actual project deliverables.

The first has to be completed before the project begins in order to establish the overall scope, while the second would be implemented during the development phase to keep the program safely on schedule.

Planning structures

Take the first of the above activities. If you go back a moment to Figure 2.2 in Chapter 2, the major reason for project failure in all the quoted surveys was given as 'poor user requirements'. Again, as we have already seen from the analysis put forward in Chapter 4, page 64, accurate and detailed requirements are very unlikely to be realised at the beginning of the project. Neither the developer or the client have the perception or the experience at the outset to provide an effective listing. A representative model of the actual work to be undertaken can only be confidently defined *after* the project has been completed (20/20 hindsight) although that may not help very much. In the real world, the first key activity is virtually certain to be incomplete and bug-ridden.

Now for the second one - formal control over the project activities and deliverables. Recall the various change mechanisms discussed in this chapter involving technology, people and project cultures, the out-of-proportion impacts, and the frequency of occurrence. In an ideal unchanging world, formal planning will produce effective results. However, under the circumstances discussed here, in the real world there seems to be very little possibility of ever gaining full control of the work schedule [12, 13].

The bottom line for any extended project is that the criteria for success in planning are well established, but there is only a vanishingly small chance of ever achieving them.

Planning in a changing world

There has to be a better way. And, indeed, there are a few better ways – both formal and informal. But, whichever route you go, they all cost.

Changing the corporate methodology

This is the approach that improves results by seriously changing the attitude and culture of the organisation. It is based on work first carried out by the Software Engineering Institute (SEI) at the Carnegie Mellon University of Pittsburgh. The acronym (there is always an acronym) is CMM which stands for the Capability Maturity Model. A brief overview of the topic is given in the appendix. For the serious student there is the book (there is always a book) which gives both an introduction and an in-depth analysis of the subject [14].

The basic approach is to encourage the host organisation to improve its capability in developing IT-based applications. This capability is classified in five separate categories starting with 'Initial'. (It should be stated that most companies never get above this level, and their success rate with IT projects is correspondingly low.) This is no light-weight conversion and calls for a lot of commitment from the organisation intending to improve its capability. The costs will usually include:

❑ Adopting a disciplined long-term development strategy;

❑ Changing the processes and procedures across the organisation;

❑ Purchasing some heavy-duty software development tools.

The overall costs will be in the band of £1000s per worker, but the return is said to be considerably above that. It is almost inevitable that, additionally, you will need a friendly consultant organisation to offer you a helping hand through the transition [15, 16].

This approach is powerful, but is only for those who make very heavy demands on their system development resources and who can handle the start-up costs and the long transition period.

Modifying the project format

Another, simpler approach is to change the nature of the projects such that the problems do not arise in the first place. This is part of the 'think-small' class of operation which recommends small development projects evolving from application to application. The idea is to limit development projects to, say, a six-month duration and deliver *something* to the client at the end of this time. Reviewing this chapter, it will be seen that most of the problems discussed will disappear if relatively short-term programs are undertaken.

The down side is that it means throwing out the SDLC (see Chapter 1 for using SDLC and Chapter 9 for discussion on discarding it). The prime advantage is that the client may end up getting something useful [17].

Altering the style of planning

This involves the recognition that long-term projects will never be stable enough to be successfully managed by structured planning techniques. We are talking about generic open-ended situations where the future is totally uncertain (high change environment) and formal planning becomes a meaningless mantra.

So what can be done in this situation? A fluid situation (technology, strategy, marketplace) will call for a fluid response. You stop anticipating and just try to handle the events as they turn up [18, 19].

> Consider the commute problem in urban centres. Every day, during the rush-hour, you take the tube/subway/metro/u-bahn (whatever). In the good old days when the equipment and track were properly maintained you planned the shortest route using interchanges and looked up the arrival and departure times in the timetable. You then left home to catch the specified train at the specified time. In less happy times, add 30 to 45 minutes to the schedule and just turn up at the station. Depending on conditions, you take the first arriving train on any route which more or less goes in your direction. At each change location, you make further on-the-spot decisions as to the best way to continue. Which may involve taking a bus, walking, etc.

At the commercial level, it means that each decision may be approached as a trial or test exercise. If you cannot get timely delivery for a laser printer, explore if an ink-jet is available and if it will it offer satisfactory performance. (Maybe not, then go on to evaluate the possible solution of using a foreign product.) The trade-off is the added stress of never knowing what tomorrow will bring against the confidence that you can box your way out of any corner. Program Management will no longer be listing activities with allocated times-to-complete. Instead, at each milestone, it will offer the current choices and options available to achieve the desired goal. One view is that this commercial freedom can be exhilarating, the other is that it is uncertain and highly stressful. Or both. Over to you.

Going down this route will involve severe changes in corporate culture and decision making processes. All the parties will have to accept a very different approach to planning where most events are *ad hoc* and unstructured. The book by R. Stacey [18] gives a convincing argument for the strategic need to adopt this approach and how best to achieve it.

Summary

We have come a long way from conventional planning in a development project. The reasons for this change are basically related to four conflicting factors that constitute an over-riding problem with formal planning:

❑ Large software systems have long development cycles and require extensive planning to control costs, resources, equipment and priorities;

❑ Planning, by the very nature of the exercise, seeks to undertake future activities in a controlled, rational and effective manner. Without such planning, most projects would rapidly descend into chaos;

❑ For planning to be meaningful, the future should be sensibly known and unchanging. Where changes do in fact occur, they should be of a limited or anticipated nature and without rapid transitions; but

❑ Long duration software projects suffer from major, unforeseen and generally rapid changes. These are due to (among others) development setbacks, migration of personnel, economic down-turns, strategic reversals, modified technology and revised end-user expectations.

References

1 Website: http://navismagazine.com/sample/xxi-cent-warships/degaulle.htm
2 Bell S, France's prestige warship all at sea, The London Times, 25.2.1999, p.20
3 Byte Magazine, March 1989
4 Personal Computer World, June 1989
5 Yeates D (ed), System Project Management, Pitman, 1986, Chapter 3
6 Bentley C, Introducing PRINCE, NCC Blackwell, 1992, p.1
7 Donnelly F, Plan for all seasons, Computing, 4.6.1992, p.32
8 Kavanagh J, Blind leading the blind into IT fog, Interface, The London Times, 6.8.1997, p.10
9 Gulton A, Managing the unexpected, Computer Weekly, 4.3.1999, p.30
10 Belford C, Integrated Business Software Systems: The Cost of Change, Executive Brief, website: www.govcomp.com/executivebrief.html
11 Collins T and Bicknell D, Crash, p.378, *(see under Bibliography)*
12 Bicknell D and Vowler J, IT projects failing to reach for the sky, Computer Weekly, 10.12.1998, p.12
13 Probert C, When time is the application's enemy, Computer Weekly, 10.12.1998, p.28
14 Humphrey W, Managing the Software Process, Addison-Wesley, 1989
15 LBMS, Process Management – Optimising Software Development, *(see under Documents)*
16 Jones C, Software Project Management in the 21st Century, American Programmer, February 1998
17 Gilb T, Building Evolving Software, Software Management Magazine, July 1989, p.28
18 Stacey R, Dynamic Strategic Management for the 1990s, p.24 , *(see under Bibliography)*
19 Glass N, Chaos, Non-linear Systems and Day-to-day Management, European Management Journal, Vol.14, No. 1, February 1996, p.98

Chapter 6 Forecasting

The conventional view

This chapter will examine the fundamentals of project management (PM) as it is applied to large system development. The various key aspects of PM such as work and resource estimating, schedule planning and control, along with budget allocations and spend monitors, will all be assessed here. Together, they provide the third vital support for new system projects – as shown in Figure 6.1.

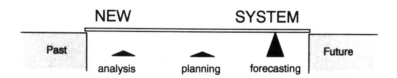

Figure 6.1 The underpinning of new systems

The standard sources on project management, up to the present time, continue to recognise the difficulties and irritations of using these disciplines, but do offer a number of panaceas and soothing unguents to relieve the corporate pain. Accurate models allowing true forecasting are harder to come by, but some modern approaches will be addressed later. But perhaps we should start with the traditional package.

The project manager role

Many times over the life of the project, PM will have to interface with senior management, line managers, end-users, design engineers, accountants, quality and test teams, HR planners, training personnel, plant supervisors and operational staff. Among others. And each one will expect his or her specific objectives to be treated on a top-priority basis. Furthermore, when the news is not so good (and the news is frequently not so good) it is pretty much standard practice to shoot the messenger.

The qualities needed for providing good PM is indicated in the 'wish-list' of Figure 6.2. where some of the skills required weekly – perhaps for years at a time – are listed. In general terms, this is often a difficult, thankless and challenging job.

Figure 6.2   PM – the role

Start-up check list

It may not be possible, but it is certainly very desirable to have a clear idea of what is to be expected from the project activities and who will deliver them. In other words, to have answers to the following questions:

❑ What is the overall budget that has been agreed?

❑ What is the maximum anticipated timescale for a successful implementation of the system?

❑ What staff (and skills) will be available for the project?

❑ What commercial hardware and software is intended for use in the system?

❑ What is the proposed development methodology?

❑ What is the status and availability for, say, the functional specification of the system?

❏ What is the intended quality level, i.e. what sign-off procedures will be implemented, what documentation will need to be generated, what test strategy will be applied?

❏ What defined deliverables (hardware, software, documentation, training, and support) are to be handed over to the user?

However, note that even if this data is defined and available from the start, the probability of the given figures remaining valid (for more than, say, three to six months) is always going to be rather low.

The project management activities

There are three key features of project management:

❏ Much like the entire development program, PM is basically about people. Ideally, it relates to a team, or teams, whose members work harmoniously and effectively to achieve some common goal. In this case, the goal is mainly interviewing, reporting to, and interfacing with, other members of the organisation involved in some project activity;

❏ A project is temporary – that is, it is intended to be finished and completed at some designated point. Whatever the technical, political or strategic objectives, PM concerns itself primarily with issues of start and end-dates and the means to achieve them;

❏ The scope of the overall forecasting exercise relates to initiating and tracking the following processes:

Estimating   Assessing the probable development time span for each of the planned project sub-elements;

Scheduling   Providing a comprehensive time plan taking into account all the required activities and related corporate resources;

Costing   Lies, damn lies and costings. How to assemble and maintain a project budget proposal that is acceptable to senior management.

The standard approach

For any new development plan, the first use of PM comes at the end of the feasibility study. In pulling all the data together, the provisional estimates of resource and schedule application are injected into the business plan for approval by some higher authority. This is the document which essentially addresses some variant of the formula:

Value = Corporate benefit - Development cost

In the nature of things, the right-hand side nearly always turns out to be significantly positive – regardless of any subsequent outcome.

The second phase comes with the main 'analysis' activity. At this point, some in-depth reviewing of the project occurs and the planned activities come under serious scrutiny. The itemised schedules, the personnel needs and the overall costs project cycles are refined until again acceptable to senior management. The sign-off duly occurs, funds are released, and the whole vast stream-shrouded project engine shudders into life for its few brief years of existence.

The final phase lasts for virtually the rest of the development, where PM is used to monitor the status of the project on some regular reporting basis. This status is compared with the original planned figures and if any serious discrepancy should occur, the problem is reported upwards. Conversely, PM can be used to identify the impacts and knock-on effects of changing existing priorities, activities and resource allocations.

So far, all very normal and reasonable.

Modern methods

In the 60s and 70s, whole check lists were assembled and formalised – estimate this, add that, schedule the total, move on to the next item. Up to a point it worked. However, even now it is still generally agreed that estimating is mainly an 'art' and tends to be an uncertain mix of prior experience, if applicable, and guesswork [1]. Most models used to develop estimates are based on estimated lines of code, LOC, or KLOC (yes, estimates on estimates) and these models are all empirically derived [2].

From another angle, some utilities were developed that would allow you to graphically analyse the status of the project:

❑ Gantt charts, or bar charts, can be applied where only a limited number of variables are under review. These can get fairly meaningless with, say, 60 upwards lines of input. For these more complex conditions use PERT;

❑ PERT (Program Evaluation and Review Technique) can still be used as a tool for creating network views of the larger project where priority milestones are identified through 'critical path' analysis [3]. But, basically, estimating still remains an art-form.

Incidentally, reference 3 is a good general introduction to Information Technology for students and senior managers. It has three key advantages: it is written in a clear and simple style; it is big, i.e. covers a lot of ground; and it is relatively cheap.

Throughout the 80s and 90s, the estimation industry started to get better – or, at least, more expensive.

PRINCE

This project tool (PRojects IN Controlled Environments) has been more or less promoted over the last two decades as a suitable companion to the planning methodology SSADM (Structured Systems Analysis & Design Methodology). SSADM is largely applied in the UK as a system development methodology (see the reference material in the appendix) and is actively supported by UK government institutions. It is firmly based on the structure of the SDLC discussed in Chapter 1.

This is a formal, highly structured project management tool. The objective is to enable projects to be completed on time, within budget, and meeting defined performance criteria and this is, in theory, achievable.

Properties

The basic structure of PRINCE is intended to be portable to any project and the principal aim is to establish a set of deliverable products [4]. The planning then defines all the steps needed to develop these products and to track every step as it is implemented.

The main features of this tool are:

❑ User participation in ongoing developments and upgrades;

❑ Formal role assignment of project workforce;

❑ Procedures for signing-off activities and risk minimisation;

❑ Framework for inter-disciplinary meetings and agreements;

❑ Full conformance to BS 5750, the UK quality standard.

All this goes along with a structured and well-defined project format which will be conformed to in all applications.

Much like SDLC, there is a high service overhead (i.e. the provision of reporting procedures, control mechanisms and management tools to assist the main thrust of system design), the cost of which has to be carried by the system development funding. On this basis, the formalism is best suited to very large projects where this added service cost will be a relatively small proportion of the total budget.

COCOMO

This is a modelling tool to quantify the overall project man-months with some accuracy. The COnstructive COst MOdel was first developed by Boehm in the early 80s [5], and then upgraded to COCOMO II in the mid-90s. A number of derived software packages including the application COCOMO II have subsequently become available.

It is based on three levels of detail (i.e. increasing amount of data to be estimated at the higher level with a corresponding improvement in overall accuracy). At each level, certain appropriate parameters have to be estimated and then plugged into the working equation for each defined activity. The output of the equation will determine the activity man-months that will ultimately be needed:

❑ Basic: the key parameter here is the estimated size of software deliverables;

❑ Intermediate: extended model to include such parameters as estimates of analyst capability and product complexity;

❑ Detailed: yet more added parameters for estimation.

Another factor which will affect the final figures is the development mode of each project. This is a representation of the relative 'difficulty' of the project framework:

❏ Organic: a small project in a benign and familiar environment;

❏ Semi-detached: more challenging, more risky projects, say, a system for a global bank;

❏ Embedded: high quality, high performance, say, a nuclear station system or a space-vehicle module.

The decisions about the 'level' and the 'mode' for the project are made, and the activity estimates are prepared. This leads to a full set of project man-month estimates which, in turn, will be used to determine the workforce requirements. From there, it is a short step to the overall cost figures.

EVMS

This particular project tool (Earned Value Management System) is based on work initially carried out in the 60s by the US Department of Defence [6]. The initial objective was to enable procurement programs and outside contractor's work to be evaluated on a secure basis, but it has since evolved into a powerful check on the status and ongoing viability for any development program. Over the years it seems to have established an enthusiastic following in a number of countries for big defence projects, and a reasonable number of related articles have been published [7].

In conventional project management, the status of the development program is related to whether individual activities have been completed or not. PERT techniques enable *slippage* or *time-to-complete* estimates to be generated, but there is no budgetry model for comparison purposes. In EVMS, the actual *value* of the work done at any one time is compared to the original estimated planned value. This allows effective early warning of deviation of real-world development performance compared to the original target figures. Used in this way it can act as a risk-management tool.

The assumptions are that:

❏ You can totally identify all the activities that will have to be undertaken in order to deliver the final product to the client;

❏ In terms of cost, either financial or time-to-complete (which are largely interchangeable), you can allocate an actual cost value to each of the above defined activities.

Once that has been achieved, then a full bottom-up plan can be generated and maintained. The basic diagram is given below in Figure 6.3 where the shaded area represents the work still to be carried out. The top, diagonal dotted line in the figure is based on the above two assumptions being met. It gives the original forecast estimate of the cost parameter (say man-months) required to complete all the elements of the project. Wherever it crosses the current time marker, in this case the t = 50% line, the equivalent cost parameter figure (represented by the related grey horizontal line) will indicate the current *planned costs* of the work done to that point.

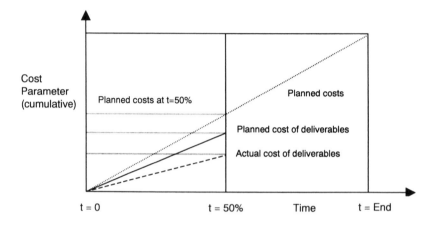

Figure 6.3 The basic earned value model

The second, solid line shows the planned costs that were forecast for the deliverables (i.e. actual work modules developed and completed) at the time of measure, in this case at the 50% time marker. This current value is given by the middle grey line and is defined as the *earned value*. Since this line is *below* that generated by the dotted line parameter, the planned costs, this indicates that *less* work has been carried out to date than was originally envisaged. Clearly this implies a schedule slippage, which will need to be addressed.

The bottom, dashed, line displays the cumulative recorded costs for the work carried out – the *actual costs*. Compared with the solid line, the recorded costs for t = 50% are seen to be *less* than the planned costs for the delivered modules. For once this is reporting good news, since it indicates that there is still some unspent funds in the program.

To summarise the situation at any one time:

Schedule Performance   = earned value – planned costs   {should be positive}

Cost Performance   = earned value – actual costs   {should be positive}

Monitoring these two performance parameters at regular time intervals will provide a useful picture of the continuing status of the project. In the example above, the schedule status is evidently poor while the cost situation is seen to be good. It is worth noting that this approach has been recommended as particularly suitable for software projects [8].

Problem areas

The coverage to date has been relatively upbeat and positive, so perhaps it would be reasonable now to take a look at the dark side. Let's start with another small example to illustrate what happens in the real world.

> In 1989, priority was given by the UK Crown Prosecution Service (CPS) to the development of a new Information Technology package. It would generate and upgrade legal case statistics, provide performance and management information and standardise the related case documentation. This package, the Scope case tracking system, would replace a number of obsolete procedures and would become operational in the 1993-1994 timeframe. It was targeted to cost £8 million.

> In 1990, the CPS reported to the Committee of Public Accounts that the development was due to be piloted in late 1991 and was still planned to be completed in 1993-1994.

> In 1997, just over half the CPS branches had the system installed (the users reporting unsatisfactory performance). The total cost in 1997 had grown to £9.6 million; the overall total was going to rise to £15.9 million; and on top of this there were additional projected expenditures in the pipeline put at £6 million [9].

By the end of 1997, the CPS recognised that the existing system was too outdated to be applied and it was decided to plan and develop an entirely new system [10].

In effect, the CPS had spent just under £10 million over 8 years for a cancelled project. Looking over the above data, we have to ask the inevitable question:

What is the relevance of project management to real projects?

In other words, why should anyone care what estimating accuracy is claimed, what budget-fixing mechanism is used, or what status-reporting strategy is adopted? If the eventual historical result is about 100% over both budget and schedule estimates (which definitely occurred in the above case), why bother going through the motions?

One could further investigate this project to seek specific reasons why it crashed so convincingly. Alternatively, we can look at the generalities of project management to establish the fault lines that exist in virtually all cases where the scale of activities are spread over a number of years.

Working environment

Before we start looking at the real matters of interest, it may be worthwhile keeping in mind the following three central points:

Feasibility

For most large projects, it is virtually impossible to establish all the key activities, development tools or project requirements at the start-up of the development process (see Chapter 4).

Planning

For most large projects, it is virtually impossible to implement any effective planning envelope for the exercise. If the key activities are poorly defined (above) then the time required to undertake these activities has to be largely unknown. In any case, once the project is underway, the impact of ongoing changes will make the planning control highly unreliable (Chapter 5).

Estimating

For most large projects, it is virtually impossible to generate a meaningful schedule and cost model. This is the biggest single obstacle in the project business and most companies still do not seem able to rise to this particular challenge [11, 12].

General rules for PM

Very often, the basic problem is that arbitrary senior management decisions tend to determine the course of the project. This will occur with leaders in industry, public service, military or local government (see Chapter 7).

Take another look at the Scope project above, and try to understand the person, task force or committee who sanctioned and continued supporting this project. (It is certainly far from unique: the UK Prison Service recently laid out more than £8 million for a feasibility study by a variety of consultants. It took two years and the proposed Quantum project was then cancelled. That is to say, it was decided to continue the project, but in another way [13].)

It is not difficult to put together a simple list outlining the problems of Project Management. For example, the presence of any of the following factors is very likely to destroy any new planned project:

❏ There is an immovable deadline, say, the introduction of a new banking system or a satellite launch window;

❏ The project is deliberately underestimated in order to make a bid that will undercut the competition;

❏ The work is labelled one or more of the following: state-of-the-art, quantum-leap, new generation, advanced technology, high-level integration.

❏ The analysts lack experience in the application, culture of the organisation, existing project standards, or workforce skills;

❏ Top management, marketing, etc., insist on developing a particular project with a given deadline, for their own good reasons;

❏ Features and constraints are added to an existing project without any upgrade to the budgets or schedule figures.

Impact of errors

The above few pages have shown that there are still some unresolved problems with conventional PM reporting. Inadequacy, complexity, interference, and fear of competition: these are often the unwanted companions of any start-up project. And what is the knock-on effect of forecasts made under these conditions?

Underscoping

A true one year project will call for, say, 1/3 of the time, or 4 months for development. If only 6 months is artificially allocated for the overall project then the time for development, now 2 months, will be grossly insufficient.

Management

Time that should be spent on project related matters will now be spent arguing with other parties, defending the last status report, promoting the latest current schedules and begging for the latest rumours from the lab. And this is going to occur every month.

Truncation

Overspend on early activities (design) will tend to cause downstream activities (test, documentation) to be foreshortened.

Performance

When serious delays arise, the number of design features will be cut down or the testing phase will be reduced. This will reduce design time and cut back some of the schedule slippage.

Overtime

Working in a crisis environment is stimulating in the short term, but extended periods of long work hours are usually totally counter-productive.

Staffing levels

Importing contractor staff is a powerful project weapon if it is a *planned* import. Bringing them in to solve today's unexpected crisis tends to be an expensive non-solution.

And so it goes on. For more gory details on participating in poorly managed software projects get hold of the book 'Death March' – but it is not for the faint-hearted [14].

Specific problems with specific tools

A quick look at the downside of the control and modelling tools discussed in the previous section.

PRINCE

This is the highly structured project management tool used with the SSADM program which has been extensively discussed in Chapters 5 and 9. And the formalised approach has the same inexorable logic applied to the probable casualty rate:

❑ Highly structured programs call up high overhead costs;

❑ High overhead costs can only be absorbed in large projects;

❑ Large projects take a number of years;

❑ Changes over years kill highly structured programs;

❑ Q.E.D.

COCOMO

The model that calculates the time-to-complete for each activity via a first estimate of 'lines of code'. However, Chapter 4 shows that this estimate cannot be made with any confidence at an early stage [15].

❑ Involves correct decision on 'level' and 'mode';

❑ Depends on 'lines of code' estimates at outset. Accuracy likely to be low;

❑ Requires serious culture change in organisation. Takes time.

EVMS

The tool that captures the value of the work done to date and compares it with the original estimates. But, as reference 6 indicates, there are still problems which will need top management support to handle:

❑ If reporting slow (months not days), it has little value;

❑ Number of monitored parameters is still too high (32);

❑ Needs 100% activity capture at the outset. Which is unlikely;

❑ High start-up cost, learning cost, and overhead cost.

It *is* possible to use EVMS to good effect. But it will almost certainly take a lot of time and effort; a willingness to experiment and modify the means of application; and probably the support of the entire organisation to move up the SEI/CMM levels (see Appendix 2) [16].

Value

There is one little piece of unfinished business left – the question of value. Later on in Chapter 12 we shall look at the parameter as it is applied to the whole development project. However, in this instance we are simply concerned with the equation defining value, given earlier in the chapter, which can be used in the business plan.

Value for the business plan

The equation given on page 86 involves two parameters, 'Corporate benefit' and 'Development cost'. And therein lies a bit of a problem. Just how do you set about quantifying these parameters?

Corporate benefit

OK, let's go for the jugular. Just what is this 'corporate benefit' thing? It (or something meaning pretty much the same thing) is a term used by the majority of strategists, consultants, and serious financial analysts. Most people will say, yes, I know the term. However, for all that, can anyone define it, quantify it, test it, enhance it, market it? What are the units of measure? How do you benchmark one proposal against another in terms of relative corporate benefit? For example, in a fast changing world, how do I compare the merits of developing a £1 million intranet against the investment of £1 million for a marketing campaign? What was the perceived corporate benefit of the Scope case tracking system?

One view says that it is currently not possible to quantify the advantages of, say, information management, but that you should go out and make it happen anyway [17]. On the other hand, some views suggest that bottom line justification for IT products is the only way forward for secure corporate investment [18, 19]. Yet another approach is to formally establish a common yardstick in the organisation with respect to all tangible and intangible benefits. At least this will enable different projects to be compared for comparative benefit [20].

The sad truth: there is no standard for establishing the bottom-line return-on-investment, no generic means of measuring strategic advantage. There is no industrially agreed definition of benefit. Go out and find one you like and use it. It is probably just as good and meaningful (or as bad and meaningless) as the next one.

Development cost

Everyone is fine on costs. Costs can be measured and recorded. Costs are what the developer spends. No problem here.

Let's consider any project that was completed, or cancelled last year in *your* organisation. Now see if you can find anyone who can tell you the overall cost of this project. Do not ask for a full written break-out of costs unless you are the chairman, CEO or VP (it will take an enormous amount of work to deliver), but see if such permanent records are, in principle, available. Make sure you ask for coverage of all expenses incurred by the participating departments in the organisation and by all the different outside parties. This should include the cost of all related travel-time, meetings, office rental and other expenses, documentation, audits and reviews, organisational services, such as the crèche or medical centre, system test activities, project management, communication facilities, training, and hardware/software purchase, installation and maintenance. My guess is that an overall figure will be forthcoming (much like that given for the Scope project above) but a hard-nosed review of costs will nearly always show that there are inadequate procedures to capture all the costs. Go on, give it a try. And if you can come up with the relevant figures, your company is clearly in great shape. For all that, it will almost certainly be in a minority, as few organisations have the all the facilities and procedures (or the inclination) in place to monitor such detail [21].

Business plan

In the last few paragraphs we have briefly reviewed the mechanics of providing bottom-line figures for corporate benefit and development cost. Notice that in generating these figures for both of the above parameters, it is exceedingly hard to provide any working accuracy *even looking back, after the event.* Now consider the problem of estimating these figures at the start of a program which is due to take a number of years to implement. Recall:

❑ No-one can foresee all the hardware components or specification items or the actual application or any perceived benefit of the final installed product a few years down the line (ask the French Navy);

❑ Equally, it will be difficult to quantify the breakdown of the project into all its work units and to estimate the corresponding costs;

❑ And virtually impossible to anticipate the inevitable changes that will modify the original program in some unforeseeable manner.

Summing up this section, there is little chance that any useful figures for either the assumed corporate benefit or the estimated cost factor will be available at the start of the project. Which reduces any business plan to a gigantic act of faith.

Summary

There are four key areas that have been covered here in terms of managing long-term development exercises with conventional PM.

❑ Large software systems will require professional project management to generate activity proposals, control development costs, optimise the use of personnel and equipment and to report status to senior management.

❑ Modern methods have been proposed as significantly improving the forecasting and control capability of the project manager:

- PRINCE   : Provides a structured project environment;
- COCOMO : Enables the cost of activities to be estimated;
- EVMS   : Compares current status against the original targets.

❑ Virtually all modern PM monitoring processes require that:

- All the activities to be implemented are known at the outset;
- The cost of such activities have been accurately estimated.

Neither of these criteria are likely to be achievable for the vast majority of new projects.

❑ The first important action in starting up any new project is generating a business plan for overview and acceptance by senior management. Since the plan is based on an initial study during the feasibility phase (or perhaps later during analysis), the probability that the plan will contain any useful long-term data is very low.

References

1 Yeates D (ed), System Project Management, Pitman, 1986, p. 83

2 Pressman R, Software Engineering: A Practitioner's Approach, McGraw Hill, 1982, p. 75

3 Knott G and Waites N, Information Technology, Business Education Publishers, 1995, p.658.

4 Bentley C, Introducing PRINCE, NCC Blackwell, 1992, p.10

5 Boehm B, Software Engineering Economics, Prentice Hall, 1981

6 Major Acquisitions – Significant Changes Underway in DOD's Earned Value Management Process, United States General Accounting Office, GAO/NSAID-97-108, May 1997

7 Website: www.acq.osd.mil/pm/paperpres/paperpres.html

8 Fleming Q and Koppelman J, Earned Value Project Management, website: www.stsc.hill.af.mil/crosstalk/1998/jul/value.html

9 Crown Prosecution Service: Report by the Comptroller and Auditor General, National Audit Office, HC 400 Session 1997-98, 12 December 1997, p. 12, 29

10 Prosecution service to ditch late legal system, Computer Weekly, 18.12.1997, p. 3

11 Brooks F, The mythical man-month, Chapter 2, *(see under Bibliography)*

12 Pengelly A, How long is a piece of string?, The Computer Bulletin, March 1998, p.14

13 Phillips S, Prison Service wastes £8m after dropping IT overhaul, Computer Weekly, 8.4.1999, p.821

14 Yourden E, Death March, *(see under Bibliography)*

15 O'Brien B, Information Management Decisions, p.242 , *(see under Bibliography)*

16 Lipke W, Applying Management Reserve to Software Project Management, website www.acq.osd.mil/pm/paperpres/lipke/lipke_art.html

17 Vowler J, How do you know when the price is right in measuring knowledge?, Computer Weekly, 17.9.1998, p.56

18 Palmer D, Justifying it, Computer Bulletin, December 1994, p.24

19 Mathieson S, Analysts clash over US report, Computing, 10.7.1998, p.2

20 Gurton A, The bottom line, Information Age, September 1997, p.14

21 Wilson M, The Information Edge, p.98, Pitman Publishing, 1997

Chapter 7

Partnership

Status review

This chapter is in the nature of a wrap-up session. It will conclude Part 2 by looking at some of the lesser dangers to a system development project (as small Piranha fish may be considered less dangerous than their larger brothers). But first we can take a look at the current situation.

Recall that the objective of this section has been to explore the means of crossing from the old system to the new using a design bridge of sufficient strength and adequate underpinnings. However, the last few chapters have consistently shown that there are no effective supports to such a bridge in terms of analysis, planning or forecasting (Figure 7.1).

Figure 7.1 The non-underpinning of new systems

Without these supports, which are conventionally taken for granted, the only rational expectation is for a high failure rate in crossing over from the old to the new system. The surveys and actual case histories of system projects which were covered in Part 1 simply act to confirm this expectation. The goal for this chapter will be to establish the impact of these failures on the main parties involved and to examine the likely outcomes. But first, let's try and understand the scope of the problem.

Process cycle

There are a considerable number of different people with different skills involved in a system development. But, for our purposes here, we can trim them down to just two principal roles: the client and the developer. These are the ones that form the basic working 'partnership' of this chapter's title and it is this partnership that will be severely at risk when the development edifice finally crashes a few years further down the line. The 'crashing' is an assumption, but, from Chapter 2, it seems a reasonable one to make – especially for the larger projects. The transition from the first smiling agreement to the terse decision to cancel, from the dream to the nightmare, is a common enough experience in real life, but it has not been well captured in a modelled form. There are no basic engineering principles to be applied here, no technology products – just human interaction on a readily repeatable scale. But it is important to understand what happens to the project as a result.

The start-up model

At the point of formalising a partnership to create a new commercial system, it all looks very promising – see Figure 7.2.

❑ The x-axis represents *time* in some suitable unit, say 'months' or 'years'. The y-axis has two possible alternative modes: that of *cost* (units of mega-dollar, giga-franc or whatever) and, at the same time, as a measure of completed, tested and documented parts to date – i.e. *modules* of hardware or software elements. (In crude terms, the number of modules can be taken as a measure of the required end-product performance. As more performance features are called up, they will tend to require more modules to implement them.)

❏ The dashed lines represent agreed target values. The hand-over will occur in so many designated years (months) and this is shown by the vertical dashed line. The overall cost and number of modules will be represented by the horizontal line, i.e. so many dollars etc. for so many modules of the system. The 'agreed level' will relate to appropriate figures for both these parameters, and the point where the two dashed lines meet will constitute the end of the project.

❏ The full line represents the actual normalised flow of both the costing and the module activity over time as more and more modules are delivered for an increasing cost.

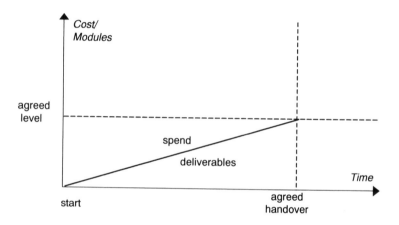

Figure 7.2   The basic activity plan

This is the position seen at the beginning of the project, at the $t = 0$ marker. This is the point where the feasibility studies have been carried out and the first system analyses have been completed (Chapter 4). The activity plot looks simple enough and this is the champagne-popping, back-slapping and everyone-is-going-to-make-a-killing sort of time.

The review

A few months or years go by. The developers have learnt a great deal about the overall technical problems, and are finally prepared to define more accurately their new schedule time and cost estimates (upward, ever upward). In the other corner, the client now has a much better understanding of what is possible and what he/she *really* wants from the new system. As a result, the agreed modules will be in for some serious modifications to enhance the utility of the planned product (Chapter 5).

At this point a formal review is usually set up. Both parties bring their upgrades and new requirements to the meeting and they eventually thrash out a revised agreement.

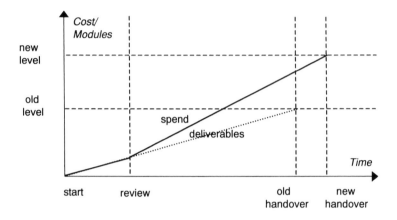

Figure 7.3   The revised activity model

This new state can be represented by Figure 7.3. which shows the agreed new planning position as a result of the review. So many extra modules will now cost so much more money (upper dashed line), and all this will delay the project by so many time units to the new hand-over date (rightmost dashed line). The original objective is shown by the dotted line while the revised plan is indicated by the new full line. There are still some smiles, although they may be looking a bit strained by now.

Development reality

There may be one or more of the review meetings shown above, giving one or more revised project targets. However, sooner or later the developer gets down to some serious work. Hardware gets reviewed and purchased, specifications are signed off and software lines of code get written and tested. A number of months/years go by with some corresponding deliverables being completed and some cost figures arrived at. These parameters are monitored by the Project Management group (see Chapter 6) and at some point it becomes obvious that a genuine problem exists. The position is now shown in Figure 7.4. The normalised value for costs, 'spend', has gone screaming up (upper full line) from the target level (dotted line). At the same time the normalised value for completed modules, 'deliverables', has sagged badly from the agreed figure to a much lower value (lower full line). The project is rapidly running out of control and, sooner or later, someone is going to have to pull the plug. Or throw really big money at it. Or kill the functionality.

Figure 7.4 is a simple graphic model which represents the typical project in the process of breakdown. It shows the first estimates, the upgraded and revised target figures and then, finally, what is actually happening to the project, compared to what was *planned* to happen, as the project evolves in real life. It is a generic model, i.e. it is pretty much the standard course of events to be expected from the majority of large software development projects. Check it out: compare this model evolving pattern to the real projects discussed in Chapter 3. Nearly all of the system case histories covered there will fit the pattern.

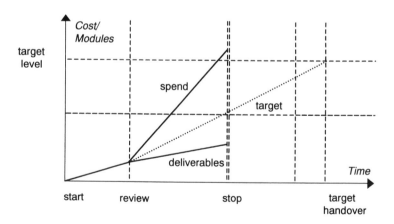

Figure 7.4 The project development model

Conversely, carry out a simple conformance check by going over some of your own company's previous/current projects. Do not worry about the details, just look for the general shape.

Reverting to Figure 7.4 once more, we see that virtually all software projects (much like all other living entities) can be conceptually defined by three basic functions: the formal start-up; the system development activity; and the project shut-down. In our case, this will broadly correspond to a) the selection of a partner formalised by the signing of a contract; b) the corporate co-operation and commercial inter-working phase; and c) project cancellation with what is often a common terminating activity: some sort of dispute resolution. Poor handling of each of these three functions could further degrade what is already a major high-cost high-risk exposure situation. As such, it should be clear that these topics are all strategic and each of them will need to be treated accordingly, i.e. call for serious continuing involvement by the senior management.

After these functions have been discussed, the closing section will summarise one other important aspect of selecting partners that has not been considered up to now: the identification of a potential disaster partner – i.e. one that contains *kamikaze management*. This refers to the senior decision-makers who, without any assistance from others, can pull the entire system development project down into ruin and perdition. A one-man walking-disaster team.

The contract

The start-up is primarily concerned with the definition and subsequent satisfaction of a perceived need coming from one of the two parties (the client). For some administrative or competitive reason a new, or enhanced, or more integrated computer system is felt to be desirable by the senior management of the client organisation. This is the perceived need. As a result, this sets in motion the competitive tender phase, i.e. a number of different development groups will be invited to tender for the job (they get an RFP, a Request For Proposal). Even this can be a tricky exercise and may need some care in seeking out the *right* potential suppliers [1]. Ultimately, a partner company (the supplier) is selected from the responding candidates. The next phase comprises a further period of in-depth discussions and negotiations between the new partners. These discussions, in turn, lead to a definition of the shared enterprise – what items are to be delivered, when this should occur and how much this whole exercise will cost. This commercial understanding is then formalised into some sort of binding contract which finally releases funds into a program of work for the new project. It sounds reasonably straightforward, but, as always, there are a few hidden snags.

Preliminaries – the partner selection

Question: how easy is it to pick a wrong partner? Answer: very easy. Whether it is at the personal relationship level between two people, or commercially with departments of large international organisations, the possibility of getting it completely wrong is always there. To jog your memory, go back to Chapter 3 and then consider how you would handle some of the following possibilities for your next development exercise :

❑ The partner is about to go bankrupt or apply for Chapter 11;

❑ This supplier is not expert, but will say anything to get the job;

❑ This client never accepts the best bid, only the lowest;

❑ The supplier artificially slashes costs to beat the competition;

❑ That client does not understand the term 'design freeze';

❑ Each partner reads different objectives into the contract;

❑ The strategic consultant wants to take the day-to-day work.

It may be much more important to seek out a good match in corporate rapport and style than to worry about pure technical knowledge. You can train for technical skills but you cannot always live with a megalomaniac CEO. For a review of some 'partners-from-hell', see the later section on 'Kamikaze management'. In any case, when looking for a partner, always look out for a company which is recommended rather than advertised.

The approach to a contract

There are a number of problems with legally binding contracts – especially for the smaller organisations. They may not be familiar with such documents, or the vocabulary contained therein, or the underlying legal concepts that are invoked. However, whatever the reason, a bad contract can only engender the high probability of a bad project. Under these circumstances it is probably in everyone's interest to invest in legal professional advice and support [2, 3, 4] (and, again, always look out for a group that is recommended rather than advertised).

Definition

Each partner will need to formally define and agree all their development goals on paper. This may be the first time that such detailed project trade-offs are explored and that alone makes it a valuable experience. The more detail, the more the value.

Clarification

If you don't understand it, don't sign it. If the language is unclear, don't sign it. If the responsibilities of each side are ambiguously defined, don't sign it. Ditto for all obscure schedules, itemised deliverables, payments, penalty clauses, and product specifications.

Protection

This is less important since the use of a contract for legal purposes can be something of a complex, open-ended and questionable exercise in itself. The whole situation may have changed considerably since the contract was first signed, and the odds are that extra attachements or constraints were appended to the original legal document. And the changes could have been critical in some unforeseen way – see the later section on 'dispute'.

Elements of a contract

The items discussed and defined in the contract should be very detailed and generally relate to all or most of the following points:

❑ Overall system strategic objectives;

❑ Hardware definition;

❑ Operating systems, and bespoke or customised applications;

❑ Quality criteria;

❑ Built-in reliability, safety and security features;

❑ Performance test formats, test equipment and test data limits;

❑ Installation and maintenance procedures;

❑ Project development methodology and major design tools;

❏ Documentation: specifications, forms, reports and user tutorials;

❏ Schedule milestones and late delivery penalty clauses;

❏ End-user training programs and user support mechanisms;

❏ Definition of ownership of related intellectual property;

❏ Conflict resolution packages, insurance and risk limitation;

❏ Anticipated costs and payment methods.

It should be evident that if a topic outlined here is not included or has been deliberately kept vague, then at least all parties will have knowingly agreed not to address it.

Inter-working

This is the area where the two commercial partners happily co-operate in a sequence of planned development activities which eventually delivers an effective software system application. Another way of looking at this section is that it encompasses all the processes that lead from the first signing of the contract to the inevitable breakdown of the project – and on to possible litigation in the extreme case.

An example of poor interaction

The truth is that both these views are basically right. Independent of the sport, or whether the team is, say, the Boston Red Sox or Moscow Dynamo, a winning team is a happy outgoing group of people, whereas a losing side is fractious, introspective and open to paranoia. The condition and outlook of the individual members will say a great deal about the current team standing. If the partners of a given development project interact badly, it will give a similar message about the evolution of the development activity. One example could be the Denver Airport project (Chapter 3), but for this case we will take a look at another – the UK Ministry of Defence LITS project.

> The Logistics IT Strategy (LITS) was planned during the late 80s as a large, ambitious RAF integration program enabling close control of the storage of spare parts and providing accounting facilities at a global level. It was going to be a relatively simple transfer from an

existing application in another country and based on a professional strategic study carried out from 1990 to 1992.

1992   Work is planned to start in 1994 and finish in 2004. Some Members of Parliament found the times scales to be unrealistically and artificially elongated. An MOD spokesperson strongly defends the time scale figure [5].

1994   IBM is awarded the first part of the development contract worth about £175 million. The stated objective by the RAF is to save about £75 million a year as a result of tighter inventories [6].

1995   The climate changes. The RAF issued an ultimatum to the developer (IBM) to get the costs under control. The current IBM cost estimates were triple the RAF budget figures. The IBM spokesman was confident that IBM would keep the contract while one LITS employee said that morale was sinking sharply [7].

1996   Leaked MOD papers (*are there any other kind of MOD papers?*) suggest that the RAF are looking at ways to terminate the now £400 million contract. Meanwhile, IBM states publicly that it is happy with the good rapport that exists between IBM and the RAF. For all that, there is a general consensus that the project management is weak and needs to be improved a great deal [8].

1997   By the end of the year, the project was in deep trouble. IBM was losing serious money on the work, and the RAF was not getting the product at anywhere near the scheduled delivery. The original planned package had had to be considerably modified in the light of end-user experience (= *rework personnel + added costs + extended schedules*). In the meantime, the Treasury had taken in the assumed benefit savings by reducing related spares and personnel levels but there was no control system in place to compensate. This was nightmare country and everyone was hurting. The RAF finally did the only sensible thing: it took over the running of the project from IBM and started to reduce the objectives to manageable chunks [9].

This is by no means a full account, but some of the frustration and mistrust should have come across. And the question remains: how do organisations avoid getting into this mess and what can be done to get them out of it? (For some possible answers, see Part 3.)

The general model of inter-working

The previous paragraphs outlined one particular case of partnership breakdown. As with other projects, there may be problems related to the particular development, but there will also be generic reasons for failure. It is usually more fruitful to explore the generic reasons why this sort of development outcome should occur so often. To start things off, consider the following definition:

> **The 'inter-working' part of a project is that phase where both partners act to destroy the force and integrity of the contract.**

By way of explanation, return to Figure 7.4 where the contract is assumed to have been completed and signed off at $t = 0$. From here on, the only normal process is change and deviation. First on the scene is the formal review, where both parties agree to significant modifications to the original objectives and deliverables. This is followed by ongoing development activities which have to respond, perhaps over a number of years, to continuing pseudo-random changes. These changes will modify the client expectation, developer capabilities, corporate strategy, technological obsolescence and environmental factors (Chapter 5). Again, both parties will have little choice but to accept work-rounds to address these new problem areas. The impact will be to take the project objectives further and further from the original status identified in the contract. Ideally, each change, formal or informal, should be the subject of a related contract-upgrade procedure, but it tends not to happen. (Again, check this out in your company.) What all this implies is – at the end of the development work period, the schedule, delivered product, performance and costs all bear little resemblance to the original figures quoted in the source contract. Unless regularly modified to reflect every nuance of change, it will have become a worthless document – hence justifying the above definition.

Again, as the differences first appear and then increase, so the development team workload and stress levels will rise, the sense of 'crisis' will increasingly pervade the project and the morale of the workforce is going to deteriorate [10]. Remember, this is not the exception, it is going to be the norm for the majority of projects unless the issue is specifically addressed. Further, this generalised discrepancy between reality and the original contractual data will turn out to be a serious stumbling block for the next section.

Dispute

This is not the inevitable end process of a project, but neither is it all that uncommon. Look back again to Figure 7.4 and assume that the 'stop' button has been pressed. Further work is then halted and the outstanding problems are usually related to money: who should return how much and to whom. In addition, 'compensation' is one of those popular concepts that gets bandied around at this point. When commercial partners fall out, failing to handle the ensuing conflict effectively could prove to be an embarrassing and highly expensive waste of time. The major options, in order of increasing cost, include: discussion, mediation, arbitration and litigation.

Discussion

At its most basic, this will involve the two parties simply getting together on their own and thrashing out some equitable solution to the dispute. It has a number of obvious advantages: it is cheap, it is private and it can be very fast. Conversely, the main disadvantages are: a) the two parties have to be prepared to sit down at the same table with one another; and, additionally, b) they are both prepared to compromise in an effort to resolve the problems. However hard it is, this is still the easiest route to conflict resolution and is frequently used [11, 12].

Mediation

This is more or less the same as above, with the added presence of some agreed neutral third party who is there to help the negotiations along. Ultimately, the over-riding objective is still to get resolution of the problems by the two original parties.

Arbitration

In this mode, both parties agree to the appointment of a neutral third party who will hear both arguments and then make a binding decision(s) to resolve the outstanding differences. Direct negotiations or discussions have not proved suitable and a 'ruling' will be made by the arbitrator that both parties will accept and implement. This is still sensibly cheap and private but it involves loss of autonomy by the two opposed organisations.

Litigation

Where no other solution has proved possible, there is always recourse to the courts. The law is there for the group prepared to gamble and ready to place high bets. But there is never any guarantee of winning. The client will usually claim that the developer was incompetent or misleading and the system, as installed, is unusable. On the other side, the developer will claim that the user continued to make so many changes that it became impossible to design the software. (It is a good working rule of thumb that both claims are probably valid.) Usually an argument will be based on the product not meeting some set of constraints or clauses laid out in the original contract. However, before taking any action one should, perhaps, reflect on the down side:

❏ There may be no written contract, only a verbal undertaking;

❏ The written contract may not be explicit in all (or any) areas;

❏ The end product changes may have made the contract worthless;

❏ Law is expensive (and the bigger guy will have the advantage);

❏ Law as a process can be very slow and stressful;

❏ Law is public.

To the legal outsider there is no clear pattern or precedent, you can win or you can lose:

Winner

In one famous landmark case, a local authority brought a case against a leading supplier. Because of a bug in the system software, the local taxes were set too low and there was a considerable shortfall in income. The high court judgement supported the local authority and the supplier was forced to pay damages [13].

Loser

A textile manufacturer took a system supplier to court in a case that lasted three months. At the end of this time, the manufacturer lost the case and was ordered to pay costs – which were about ten times the outlay for the original system under dispute [14].

Remember that you can also win *and* lose. You, the supplier, bring a case against a client for, say, non-payment for the installed system – and you win. The client then promptly goes into liquidation leaving you with a lot of mess to clear up. Assume anything is possible in law and you won't go far wrong.

Kamikaze management

As discussed above and in Chapter 2, a failing project is relatively easy to recognise, but establishing the underlying cause can be more difficult. In general, there are two main reasons for project failure and these may be present in isolation or may be mixed up together:

❏ Inherent failure due to long-term project phenomena;

❏ Major defects in one (or both) of the senior management partners.

The former is the major subject of this book, but the latter is an all too common factor in the real world. A few words spent here on the characteristics of this type of management, with its built-in auto-destruct capability, may help you to avoid a potentially catastrophic partnership. On that basis, this section will look at some of the dangerous stereotypes who can fill the big black leather chair of senior management. The major types are outlined in Figure 7.5 below.

Figure 7.5 Stereotypes

Amateur

This sort of manager is generally to be found in local and central government in democracies where 'old boy' networks flourish, and anywhere else where nepotism is still a popular practice. Usually an attractive personality with good connections, but perhaps not too competent on technical matters and possibly without any real in-depth experience. Consider UK passports and their systems.

> The introduction of a new passport administration system led to a tremendous backlog of people waiting for passports to be processed. The developer said that the initial installation in Liverpool had coincided with an unusually large increase in demand. The management claimed that the new system speeded up the production of passports, while the union suggested that the exact opposite was true. A subsequent independent report severely criticised the Home Office for its incompetence and lack of imagination in generating the original system specification.

At first reading, it sounds like a fair description of the UK Passport Office in the summer of 1999 – but it isn't. It was a situation that had occurred one decade earlier [15, 16]. The staff at the time were so upset and dissatisfied with the new installed system that they refused to work with it. Lack of technical ability seems to have been the problem here. But the great passport panic of 1999 did have some unfortunate points of commonality:

> The introduction of a new passport administration system led to a tremendous backlog of people waiting for passports to be processed. The Passport Agency's operations director said that the initial installation in Liverpool and Newport had coincided with an unusually large increase in demand. The developer admitted that the new system was slower than the manual system it was replacing, but put it down largely to inexperience and the increased security checks. Under pressure to deliver, the senior managers felt they could safely ignore the recommendations from the previous exercise.

This is only the bare outline of the situation but it should provide a basic overview of the problem area [17, 18, 19]. Development failure-reduction inevitably requires that the current project managers are prepared to apply the lessons of any previous projects or experiences in the same field. In this case, over the interval of 10 years, no changes in the management approach appear to have occurred and no lessons appear to have been learnt. The results were thereby wholly predictable.

Now, as reported, this seems to be a straightforward example of a string of projects being run by amateurs. They bring their current job to some form of completion and then move on to the next challenge. Which is more or less OK. It would have been truly far worse if any of these results had been obtained by a *professional* management lead-team. That would have given some serious cause for worry. For all that, as potential commercial partners, managers who lack technical skills and who cannot learn from experience are well worth avoiding if at all possible.

Hydra

The Hydra was a snake of Greek mythology with many heads. If one head should be cut off, the Hydra would immediately grow another head to replace it. Sounds like a rotten concept for a project management team, since, at any one time, all you can guarantee is that there will be no single person in charge. As a result, there will be no agreement available on everyday crises or new or changed requirements. Examples from Chapter 3 may help to clarify this – first Denver airport then TAURUS:

> A Byzantine management structure had grown up around the overall project which meant that any negotiation for performance clarification, waivers, rights, space or airport access would be a time-consuming and frustrating exercise.

> The Bank of England appointed a committee to resolve issues and provide compromise solutions to outstanding problems. A further number of local-interest groups formed various audit and monitor bodies – still without any central leadership or direction.

If your potential partner organisation shows no particular signs of strong, well-structured, competent leadership, then, as a rule of thumb, drop the potential partner. You will end up saving a great deal of money.

Fat cat

This is the Managing Director who is fully and publicly committed to Corporate Service, Integrity and the Workforce. Unfortunately, he or she is even more committed to the £7 million share pay-back when the company can be sold off to an asset-stripper. Careful attention to sound market intelligence could save you a lot of embarrassment in the future.

Techie

Beware of the enthusiastic senior manager who feels that technical challenge and engineering ingenuity carry a special buzz that bring their own rewards.

> The classic case was Rolls-Royce which was forced to call in the receiver in February 1971. RR was the great technology icon of the UK and the fall from grace came from just one contract signed in 1968 to deliver one jet engine to one US aircraft manufacturer. The manufacturer was Lockheed and the engine was the RB 211. It required a quantum leap in performance, i.e. a quantum leap in risk, and the development funds were far from settled at any time during the project. There was, however, enormous faith and pride in RR's technical capability, so the financial side was considered less important. There was little or no risk analysis and no attempt to provide a fiscal safety net. The government was indifferent, the specification kept changing and by 1971 it was all over [20].

The moment you go overboard for state-of-the-art advanced technology without regard to the impact on the commercial viability of the organisation, you have become a serious danger and risk to your company. In terms of software projects, go back to Chapter 4:

> The FoxMeyer Drug company was based in Texas. It started up a *very* ambitious multi-million dollar project for monitoring and controlling orders from the warehouse - but the system never worked properly, the warehouse fixtures were late and ongoing errors caused further losses due to unrecoverable costs. Inside two years, this one system took the firm into bankruptcy.

If you find a potential partner who is excited by the latest technology and is determined to use it, assume he is temporarily unwell and keep well clear.

Politician

This is where the senior manager is prepared to make his decisions based purely on expediency and self-interest. And it is not his fault. Whatever happens. The classic case was the flight of the UK airship R101:

> The government team to build the R101 in 1929 was essentially the same team that had designed the R38, an airship that was built, flown

and crashed in 1921. The man running the R101 program for the Government was Lord Thomson of Cardington, the Secretary of State for Air. His previous career in the army (Brigadier General) clearly rendered him competent to address aeronautical matters. Regardless, in 1930, Lord Thomson insisted on flying to India in the just-completed Government designed airship. He apparently wanted to arrive at a conference there with all due pomp and splendour. In the meantime, the R101 had needed to undertake a major refit (including a new central buoyancy section, and new reversing engines) and it was just completed on October 1st 1930. As a result of the continuing pressure from Thomson to get the airship to India in early October:

- Trials had to be curtailed to 16 hours flying in good weather;
- With a defective engine, no full-power trials could occur;
- No bad-weather flying had ever been attempted;
- The airworthiness certificate was obtained without any formal or independent audit.

The actual weather conditions on October 4th were unusually bad. Sufficient to cancel the entire trip, but for the presence of the VIP passengers on board. In the event, the maiden voyage to India of this newly-designed and largely untested airship lasted about 8 hours before crashing in France in bad conditions at night with the loss of over 40 people – including the Secretary of State for Air [21].

Incidentally, [21] is a good read about perceived governmental competence in handling and supporting innovative developments in the 1920s and 30s. *Plus ça change...* Thomson never lived to blame someone else for the disaster. However, that was not to be a problem for the LAS bosses. Again quoting from the relevant case study in Chapter 3:

The first full installation and application of the London Ambulance Service's computerised system occurred on the 26th of October 1992. It was to prove an instant disaster and the decision to remove it was taken about 36 hours later. The report of the subsequent public inquiry outlined the following criticisms:

- The full system software was not complete, not tuned, and certainly not tested by the 26th October;
- The hardware had not been tested for high traffic conditions;
- There were no contingency plans or fallback options;
- The un-trained staff had no confidence in the system;

- The system required near perfect inputs and these were not forthcoming due to high operator stress or lack of training.

How did the management handle the problem? By the following day – the 27th October – they claimed that there was not much of a problem and no-one had been seriously affected by the last few days (actual related deaths were claimed to be in the range 20-40). They then went on to claim that an excessive number of calls were made on the days in question (not so) and that the ambulance crews set out to deliberately damage the system (ditto).

Politicians bring a tremendous drive to any project they are running, but are not always effective in making good judgements in the technical domain.

Corner-cutter

The term is self-explanatory and the results can be (and usually are) disastrous. These are the disease carriers of the management world and you have to ask yourself: would you like to work on a project with a senior management who cut corners? Three Mile Island may come to mind, but what about Bhopal?

In 1984 there was a chemical processing plant in Bhopal, India, 51% owned by Union Carbide. It produced a pesticide (Carbaryl) using a highly reactive and toxic feed chemical (Methyl Isocyanate or MIC). MIC is so reactive that it needs to be stored in stainless steel tanks at a temperature of about 0° C. In December 1984, a storage tank leaked MIC into the atmosphere. The subsequent investigation uncovered the following:

- The refrigeration unit in the tank had been switched off;
- The high temperature alarm had been de-activated;
- A sloppy procedure may have enabled water to enter the tank;
- An early change in the tank pressure gauge was not reported;
- The vent gas scrubber was on standby mode;
- The flare tower's pilot light had been removed;
- The local doctors were not trained in related treatments.

As a result of these non-checks, short-term changes, planning gaps, careless work, and short-cuts, some 3000 people were killed outright and another 250,000 people were permanently disabled [22].

When corners are cut, sooner or later the aircraft crashes, the nuclear plant malfunctions, the chemical plant pollutes the environment and the software systems always, always go down.

Summary

This chapter has taken the development outcomes and conclusions which were established in the previous chapters and applied them to the project framework. As a result, in planning any new system project, the following points should be kept in mind:

❑ Unless specific action is undertaken to the contrary, the typical long-term development program will tend to follow the activity plot shown in Figure 7.4. The bigger and more expensive the program, the more likely that tendency;

❑ Choosing a compatible, ethical and competent partner is probably the most difficult and important action in the whole project cycle;

❑ The initiating contract, *per se*, is invaluable for forcing each party to identify at the outset what they really want (or think they want) from the development activities. Its utility in the longer-term is much less clear and should not be depended on for litigation unless it has been studied carefully and still represents the required output product;

❑ The interaction between partners is often determined by the success or failure of their combined efforts. For most long-term projects, unless specific safeguards are put in place, the partners' relationship should be expected to degrade over time;

❑ Setting up agreed damage limitation programs to handle anticipated future conflicts between the partners would be an unusually wise approach;

❑ Make very sure that your potential partner does not have the operating style to destroy the proposed partnership, or the project activity, single-handed.

Overview to Part 2

Yes, it has been a fairly miserable trip. Every chapter has only intensified the sense of foreboding and lasting depression. However, there is not much point in looking for a cure if the illness, however unpleasant, has not been thoroughly investigated and accurately diagnosed. So let's broadly summarise the main findings from Part 2:

❏ *Feasibility* The feasibility study that underwrites any proposed new system project is almost certain to be inaccurate and incomplete. There are no tests available to measure how much of the existing system has been accurately captured as a model. Equally, there are no measurement criteria to establish that the current proposal is complete, is designable and will satisfy the client's future objectives;

❏ *Planning* Large projects need detailed and accurate planning for effective development to take place. For that planning to be meaningful, the environment must remain sensibly stable since any change will seriously alter the ground rules that supported the planning in the first place. For all that, long-term software development is characterised by continuous and significant change in every aspect of its environment;

❏ *Business plan* The project take-off is ultimately based on the acceptance of a business plan or its equivalent by the budget controllers. This is a document that outlines the anticipated cost of developing the new system to the company along with the related bottom-line profit or strategic advantage that will come from using it. Given the problems of feasibility and planning as shown above, it is difficult to see how any quoted figures for future development expense, or for future corporate benefit, can have any real business validity;

❏ *Program management* In order to manage the software development effectively, three parameters have to be known with some accuracy: a) the listing of all the activities that will be required to develop the system, b) the development times required to implement such activities and c) the overall cost of carrying out these activities. Only then can the funding be efficiently exercised and resources allocated correctly. However, if the original feasibility and planning statements are incorrect or incomplete, then none of these criteria will hold true;

❏ *Partnership* The effect of changes over time will very likely have a downward impact on the rate at which modules are delivered to the client. At the same time the related rework cycles will cause a major increase in costs. The effect of these two factors together will frequently be enough to shut down the project and alienate the two partners. In any case, selecting a partner is probably *the* high risk activity of the whole exercise.

References

1 Asner M, Invitation to the dance, http://govcomp.com/issues/199710/procurement.html
2 Reed C (ed.), Computer Law, Blackstone Press, 1996
3 Morley L., Never neglect the small print, Computing, 14.5.1992, p.28
4 Ward M. NCC conference puts out contract on legal confusion, Computing, 6.10.1994, p.8
5 Collins T, Intergraph slams RAF strategy, Computer Weekly, 27.8.1992, p5
6 Project Watch, SCO wins IBM approval for RAF project, Computing, 13.10.1994, p3
7 Moules J, RAF gives IBM 90 days to curb sky-high costs, Computing, 28.9.1995, p.1
8 Jones R, RAF considers bale-out over 'inept' IBM Lits management, Computing, 8.8.1996, p.1
9 Collins T, RAF chief to the rescue, Computer Weekly, 11.12.1997, p.20
10 Yourdon E, Death March, p.18, *(see under Bibliography)*
11 News item, Consultancy Price Waterhouse has reduced fee, Computing, 20.6.1991, p.2
12 Collins T, Users smell blood as ICI pays £1 million in dispute over lost profits, Computer Weekly, 16.1.1997, p.18
13 Murray I, Council wins £1m for poll tax software bug, The London Times, 4.10.1994, p.2
14 Collins T, A £90,000 system lands textile manufacturer with £1m bill, Computer Weekly, 26.11.1998, p.4
15 Smith J, 'Just obeying orders' says passport supplier, Datalink, 12.6.1989, p2
16 Smith J, Passport planning slammed, Datalink, 21.8.1989, p.3
17 Phillips S, Agency cuts checks on passports, Computer Weekly, 18.3.1999, p.2
18 Collins T, Siemens to pay up over Passport Agency crisis, Computer Weekly, 1.7.1999, p.1
19 Collins T, Passports roll-out advice was ignored, Computer Weekly, 8.7.1999, p.4
20 Bignell V and Fortune J, Understanding Systems Failures, p.145 *(see under Bibliography)*
21 Shute N, Slide Rule, Chapter 6, Heinemann, 1954
22 Fortune J and Peters G, Learning from Failure, Chapter 7, Wiley, 1995

Part 3 Solving the problem

Thou has turned for me my mouring into dancing: Thou hast put me off my sackcloth, and girded me with gladness

Psalm 30

Chapter 8

Taking stock

Introduction

We have finally entered the region where the outlook is starting to appear sunny and upbeat. Which makes a most welcome change. The whole of this section – Part 3 – is about providing various strategies, work-rounds, procedures and management practices to improve the odds of achieving system success. The objective will be to make corporate investment in system projects look a lot more attractive. Go down to your favourite bookshop and stand in front of the software engineering shelves. They will be stacked with book after book that outline the formal activities required for a successful development program. Well, we are about to join them. But there is the significant difference between this book and all the others. The listings, techniques, arguments and policies put forward in this section will be built on three fundamental premises:

❑ If a group of surveys produce broadly similar statistical results, then those results are likely to be valid. Especially if those surveys took place at different locations and at different times and were carried out by reputable international organisations (Chapter 2).

❑ Confidence in the above statistics should be readily reinforced by a sample of real-life case studies from different sectors and different countries (Chapter 3).

❑ The results of these surveys are, taken as a whole, remarkably consistent. Such consistency over time and space strongly suggests that there exists an underlying set of generic laws, rules and properties which will negatively impact development activity. This set of generic factors should be easily detected and identified for typical long-term projects (as established in Chapters 4 to 7).

System basics

As a reminder of the difficulties that have to be overcome in system development, we can briefly review the problems of long-term projects with a highly structured methodology – such as SSADM [1].

Change dependency

Independent of the ideology, it should be clear that any form of change to the environment will cause added stress, delay and redesign to the software project. It can be externally imposed with, say, new generic safety requirements against virus and worm attacks. Or it can be internally generated with, say, an added interface package to make the software integrate with other systems already in the organisation. Whether you are running with a structured methodology or RAD (see Appendix 2), whether the company is small or large, whether the software model is based on standard tools or OO (Appendix 2), change is a severe and ongoing risk. Under these circumstances, it is worth exploring the potential impact to the software in some detail.

Software redesign

This is roughly like saying, 'let's have a new gearbox' in the planning of a family car redesign. Virtually everyone knows what is being talked about, yet hardly anyone has the technical expertise to understand the enormous engineering implications of the new proposal. In the case of software, any modification or upgrade to a system will always cause an added heavy workload in the following areas:

Data   Extensions to an existing system will nearly always require new data structures. The extent and nature of this new data will have to be carefully analysed and database models upgraded to meet the new requirements;

Process   This section will be concerned with the way in which the organisation uses the new data. The customary approach is two step: first, to analyse how the existing data is handled as it is used in the organisation; second, to establish how the new extended data-set will have to be introduced to achieve the desired results;

Programming   Once again, a new model, the programming structure, will be generated to reflect the changes introduced in the 'process' section above. This will identify the main modules that will need to be implemented along with any modifications to existing modules. Following the analysis, the lines of operating code can then be developed, documented, tested and de-bugged;

Test   Every change to the software will call up a corresponding change to the test facilities, test documentation, routines, objectives, and results. And this is before any of the test sequences fails;

Documentation   Every one of the above activities will call up related documentation. This means that a whole new set of system drawings and user-documents will have to be written, assessed and signed off. The last action will be to enter all these drawings and documents into a new level of Configuration Management which seeks to maintain a full set of documents for every variant of the system.

A specific example is given in the 'Software change sensitivity' section in Appendix 2. Notice that the workload is only related to the actual production or change to the programmed software of the system and does not include related changes to the hardware, administration, design tools, security facilities, or user training.

Life cycle

Some methodologies (Appendix 2) are more stringent than others, and the highly structured ones are the least forgiving where change is concerned. To understand this, take another look at the life cycle diagram, Figure 1.1 given in Chapter 1. In an ideal world for the developer, the design would take place in three steps:

❑ Agree the design, schedule and budget details with the client;

❑ Develop the entire system – without the attendance of the client;

❑ Re-introduce the client to the new system at installation.

In other words, once the contract has been signed, the client is expected to go away and leave the developer to get on with the design in peace and quiet. At completion of the entire system program, say, three years later, it will be downloaded in one weekend onto the client's hardware to the unsolicited admiration and gratitude of the client's workforce. That is the theory, anyway.

In practice, things can be very different. Reviewing Chapter 3 will show a whole bank of projects where 'down-loading in one weekend' remained no more than a pipe-dream. A return to Figure 5.2 in Chapter 5 shows the factors that are likely to affect the planned outcome of the development work. An internal re-organisation, for example, two years into the program, can change the fundamental structure of the company, calling up radically different data-flows and end-user functions. Now take another look back at Figure 1.1 in Chapter 1. The development could well have reached the 'test' phase. The likely impact of the re-organisation is simple: a total re-design going back to the original analytical phase with a completely new development and documentation set. Added to this is a new works schedule to be drawn up by Project Management. Probable added impact: about 18 months overall. An alternative approach is to upgrade all the existing work – i.e. the currently developed plans and software – to bring it in line with the new specifications. However, this approach will probably take about three years as the project gets lost in the Sargasso Sea of repeatedly failing test exercises. The general rule of thumb with structured methodologies is that any serious change will tend to take you back to the beginning of the project.

Design freeze

The previous section looked at the brittle nature of the structured methodology, where any change can lead to a serious planning extension. The other side of the coin is the client who is forever changing the specifications as he or she sees the desirability of new and improved upgrades and facilities. In an effort to protect the project end-date, the client has to be aware of the advantage of keeping the design and objectives fixed. On the other hand, if the concept of 'design freeze' is rigorously applied to all long-term projects, this will simply invite system obsolescence. There is no good answer – this type of project nearly always leads to a no-win situation.

Key development factors

Once again, a brief reminder of the main difficulties to be found with long-running projects.

Analysis

It can take about a year for the designer to recognise and define the problem areas of what they are meant to be developing (system A). The client, meanwhile, will take about the same period to realise exactly what it is they really want (system B). A is usually not equal to B. This is why, in the real world, theatre-groups rehearse for about six months before putting on a play, why tennis players practice throughout the year before appearing in tournaments, and why pupillages and apprenticeships exists. Experience and familiarity are seen to bring their own reward. This approach has generally not found favour in the area of software design. A short feasibility study for a brand new state-of-the-art project will lead to the signing of a formal contract which, in turn, starts up the development activity. The odds that the specification defined in the contract will bear any relevance to the final delivered product can only be considered as very low.

Planning

To restate the obvious: an effective development program will need competent, comprehensive and detailed planning to ensure that resources and equipment are in the right place at the right time. However, the factors covered in Figure 5.2 will seek to nullify or make irrelevant all the details of the project planning documents. Planning can only be as good as the environmental stability of the development activity, and most long-term software projects have an environment in a state of continuous change (Chapter 5).

So, once again, there are two key problem areas: the poor quality of the initial analysis and the continuous modification required in the development process. These will both act to generate a large, adverse impact on any anticipated project success. In other words, accuracy of forecasting, budget assessment, test requirements and general project control can be expected to be severely degraded as the project progresses.

Development philosophy

It is time to take something positive out of all this, to make sure the scene is set for real ongoing triumphs. So let's take another look at what has been established about system developments so far.

Failure classification

There are two main types of failure projects with very different properties:

Losing

This forms the set of projects where the will, inclination or funding is not available for a new attack on the problem. In this case, the bad project result is left unchanged. Examples include the Denver baggage handler (Chapter 3) and the FoxMeyer Drug Company (Chapter 4).

Winning

These are the initial failure projects where a second attempt will often deliver the goods. This applies to most projects where the will and the finances exist to try a second time round. However bad the first results were, the second attempt, with sound management, will generally prove successful. The classic case is the software strategy developed by Microsoft. To take a generous view, Windows 1.0 and 2.0 were not outstanding successes. For all that, Windows 3.0 more or less wiped the board with the competition. The trick is to have the strength, both moral and financial, to learn the lessons of a bad product and to build on them. Other examples include the LAS and the Stock Exchange TAURUS projects (see Chapters 3 and 10), and the California DMV (see Chapter 3 and [2]).

From a strictly pedantic viewpoint, these projects were not cost-effective, and were ultimately shut down. However, at a more practical level, new system designs, based on the original development work, did eventually become operational. And that is surely a great deal better than nothing.

Large systems

The fundamental question was posed, as usual, by Fred Brooks who agreed that small projects are easier to plan and control than their bigger brothers. Still, he asked, how should big, long-term projects be handled [3]?

Consider, for the moment, the miracles and wonders of chaos theory. Particularly with reference to weather forecasting [4]. Assume that at some time $t = 0$, the current weather conditions, say – over Cambridge, are completely known and defined. It is sunny at 2.00 p.m. over Kings College. Then, can the weather conditions at the same location be accurately determined for 4 days forward, and for 4 weeks forward? Briefly, can we confidently forecast if it will rain on a given day next week and next month? Unequivocal answer from chaos theory – 'yes, we can' for the former, and 'no, we cannot' for the latter. What this means is that, independent of the power of the computer(s) or other analytical engines used, you will *never* be able to accurately predict the specific local weather conditions over a period of a few weeks ahead of the prediction time. The 'butterfly effect' will always introduce a pseudo-random uncontrollable factor into the result.

Back to large development projects. Can we provide a selection of management procedures and strategic mechanisms that will enable long-term software systems to be developed effectively? This is the key question that was asked more than 2 decades ago when Brook's book was first published and it has been sensibly unanswered ever since. Till now:

Large software projects can never be effectively developed.

And there is the answer. It is that simple. OK, perhaps it is not really that simple and some explanations will be necessary to take it on board.

Never   'Never' is a big word, and there will be times when a small number of such projects can be brought successfully to fruition (15% is reported from Chapter 2; 9% if only large projects are considered). But 'never' is still a good working approximation for the majority of projected long-term software development plans.

Large   The statement above is really related to 'long-term' since there are sound reasons why projects stretching over a number of years are unlikely to meet their original specifications or anticipated costs. However, the correlation between 'large' and 'long-term' is reasonably good, since no-one in their right mind would seek to develop a *small* project over a number of years. As for developing a large project in a small time interval, it sounds good – but go back and read Yourdon first [5].

Long-term   This refers to any project with a planned duration, say, in excess of one to two years. Under those circumstances, we are back to the two fundamental problems: a) the initial objectives will tend to be poorly understood and poorly determined; and b) the external and internal changes will act to increase costs and reduce progress during the development of the project.

Effective   The implication here is that the project is brought home on time and on budget (see 'failure' definitions in Appendix 2). A system can be made fully operational second or third time round – a 'winning' type of failure – but it will still constitute an unwelcome and totally unplanned addition to the corporate out-goings. It will not have been an 'effective development'.

There will always be exceptions: NASA did get someone on the moon in 1969 after nearly a decade of sustained leading-edge development. Perhaps your company is well trained in risk evaluation and is high up the SEI/CMM model (see Appendix 2). But, for the majority of commercial organisations, the above statement still remains a sensible starting point for the planning of future system developments. The importance here, as for the weather forecasting, lies in the fact that an answer exists. Like the forecasting, it is not a matter of eliminating the question – it is still there – but one of the possible solutions has been effectively removed and that is useful, since time and effort may now be concentrated on more likely and more productive approaches.

The silver mind-set

Once again, a concept taken from the Fred Brooks collection: is there a single technique or method out there (the silver bullet) that will allow successful project development to be undertaken? His answer was very direct – a firm 'no' [6].

Now let's consider an extension of this idea: the 'silver mind-set'. That is to say, a corporate approach to system development where a number of facilities may be applied (or not applied) as required and on demand in a flexible and informal manner. This could include:

❏ A modular approach to new products;

❏ Involvement and participation by senior management;

❏ A corporate culture adaptive to change;

❏ A build-up of suitable expertise and workforce training;

❏ Application of quality techniques as a cost-saving tool.

These sorts of facilities would take about two years to be introduced effectively into most organisations – but only if it were thought helpful to go down this road (see Appendix 1). In any case, taking this approach or knowingly staying with the current methods – now that is a truly strategic decision for most organisations.

Summary and objectives

This chapter has briefly reviewed the current situation in system development and has laid down the guidelines for a new and possibly more effective set of approaches. This, in turn, should lead to a better probability of successful investment in the field. The various techniques will be outlined through Section 3 and should enable system development to be undertaken with some measure of confidence in the final outcome. In particular, the following areas will be addressed:

❏ Technical procedures and assumptions. The practical environment for successful system development;

❏ Corporate structure. A review of the human resources that will need to be set up to provide adequate internal communication, competent project control and effective damage limitation;

❏ Management role. The qualities and competencies that will be called for in the non-technical senior management in order to provide strong strategic leadership in the IT development sector.

References

1 Meldrum M, Kejk M and Guy P, SSADM Techniques – an introduction to Version 4, Chartwell Bratt, 1993

2 Bicknell D, Just DOIT, with Californian flair, Computer Weekly, 11.9.1997, p.32

3 Brooks F, The mythical man-month, p.30, *(See under Bibliography)*

4 Glieck J, Chaos – Making a New Science, p.9-23, Heinemann, 1988

5 Yourdon E, Death March, *(see under Bibliography)*

6 Brooks F, The mythical man-month, p.179, *(see under Bibliography)*

Chapter 9

The new approach - things

Introduction

This is the first chapter that will begin the exploration of the concept 'the silver mind-set' – discussed in the last few pages of Chapter 8. It will have the objective of providing a set of practices and procedures which, if followed, will materially improve the odds of successfully developing a software system. No magic, and precious little novelty. But, in exchange, there will be a great deal of common-sense, which is sometimes lacking in the hurly-burly of exciting new state-of-the-art programming tools and tomorrow's technology design models. The totality of all the inputs discussed here (see Figure 9.1) will provide a solid framework for ongoing system development. We are going to lay down a philosophy.

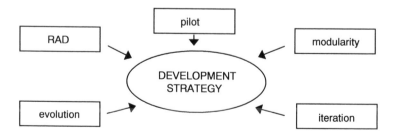

Figure 9.1   Key factors in development

Evolution

Controlling the degree of change is an important part of the overall strategy package. It is closely related to the concept of 'complexity' which measures the difference between the new system and the old one. A planned system which is dramatically different from the previous one, is going to appear very complex to the workforce which has become accustomed to the existing system. Looked at from another angle, complexity can possibly be seen as a measure of the over-riding ambition shown by the corporate leaders - the desire to build the most advanced, or the biggest or the best - and it is this ambition which is usually brought low by the Gods.

Examples

This has been touched on in the earlier chapters where, for example, the FoxMeyer Drug Company of Texas (Chapter 4) went all-out for a 'new concept' approach and all that was achieved was a bankruptcy whose reverberations are still being felt [1]. Or the baggage handling planning of Denver Airport (Chapter 3) with its extending-the-boundaries software application [2]. Again from Chapter 3, the Stock Exchange exercise, TAURUS, was initiated as an all-singing, all-dancing paper replacement exercise in handling share transactions for the London market [3]. It grew like Topsy and flew like the Titanic.

These cases, and others like them, are worth going over again and again. The bottom line is that a majority of such projects are sold to the client on the basis of significantly advancing the frontiers of technology (or management, or engineering, or whatever). The evidence in Chapter 3, and the related references in the bibliography, show very clearly that these projects are simply an invitation to flop disastrously.

So how does one handle a development with serious innovation and, at the same time, provide a strong measure of security and risk minimisation? The basic answer for most businesses is: not very well and perhaps you should not try.

Conceptual innovation

In the general scheme of things, successful companies tend to supply well-established products to well-established markets. When a smaller, neater, cheaper replacement product appears, these conservative organisations often find it difficult to make the transition to the new down-market low-priced sector. As an example, the original mainframe companies (Burroughs, Amdahl) found it virtually impossible to market a mini product which could compete with the new start-up companies in computers (Hewlett-Packard, DEC). The older companies seem to get weighed down with the excess baggage that they bring to the fight. Some current examples, possibly: will the established Barnes and Noble be able to compete on the Web with the start-up amazon.com; and, in the UK, can the internet service provider Demon Internet contain the thrust of Freeserve Ltd. from Dixons?

These examples of major new competitive ground wars are always characterised by some new innovative products which offer:

❏ A reduced performance (initially);

❏ A dramatically lower operating price;

❏ A new market niche waiting to be satisfied.

At some later date, these products will themselves evolve upwards to expand their niche penetration (desktops + network = mini).

In this situation, organisations can usually handle upgrades and minor product enhancements rather well, but major innovations or full technical replacements tend to be inherently beyond their capabilities. This rule applies not only to the evolution of computer hardware, but would appear to operate comprehensively across many other industrial sectors. Christensen's book on the industrial impact of innovation is extensive and well worth exploring [4].

Revolutionary system development

The above material seems to suggest a guideline: stick to what you know and do well, and do not try to supply or request innovative new products. Can this guideline be applied to software system development organisations? I would say yes. Consider again some of the lessons from the case histories in Chapter 3:

❏ New systems with significant planned changes from the old system do not tend to survive past the development phase;

❏ New systems using different development methodologies (change from
  Life Cycle to Object Oriented) do not tend to survive;

❏ New systems incorporating novel advanced technologies (mini to client
  server) do not tend to survive.

    In short, leave the giant leap for mankind to the heroes who can afford
it. The low-risk way to handle innovation is by linking a number of smaller,
easier leaps in succession – see the section on 'Iteration'. And should any
proposal for a sophisticated, brilliant, innovative system ever cross your in-
tray, either set up a largely autonomous entrepreneurial bunch of kids to run
it – or bin it. As a strategic policy – evolutionary, low complexity systems
may not be exciting, but they could just be attainable.

RAD methodology

The acronym stands for Rapid Application Development and it has become
an increasingly popular methodology over the last decade. For a brief
coverage see the RAD section in Appendix 2 while a more extended
discussion can be found from the bibliography [5]. Generally, it has been
applied to small projects but still needs careful handling to be effective [6].

    For better or worse, the logic is inescapable: if you want cost-effective,
operational systems to result from your development activity then sooner or
later you will have to switch over to some variant of RAD and give up the
familiar System Development Life Cycle model [7]. A basic overview of
SDLC was given in Chapter 1.

    The logical argument goes as follows:

❏ SDLC based methodologies are highly structured, fully documented,
  management heavy and resource intensive. Because of the high cost
  overheads, they are only suitable for long-term projects (Chapter 1);

❏ Long-term, large scale projects virtually always fail (Chapter 2);

❏ This is largely due to inevitable changes over time in the technology,
  customer requirements, or operating environment which will radically
  affect the final system objectives (Chapter 5).

To summarise: to have a chance of keeping to the original objectives and providing an effective solution, a new system development should ideally be small, simple and short-term. This implies, say, 9 months in planned duration, equivalent to possibly 12 months in the real world. (This approach was adopted in one project which concerned the design of a data storage scheme for patient records at the Royal Marsden Hospital in London. It had a well-defined objective and, from the outset, the scope of the exercise was kept strictly limited. And it worked [8].)

Returning to the bulleted points above, a short-term project strategy is seen to be desirable but this is simply not compatible with the SDLC methodology. The brutal conclusion is: wave goodbye to all standard methodologies based on the SDLC, including, among others, SSADM, Merise, and YSM (Yourdon System Method). Such a move constitutes a major upheaval and cannot be carried out overnight, but it can be brought into the strategic arena for future implementation. There will be more discussion on how this could be carried out in the section 'Modularity', along with the whole of the next chapter.

For a number of medium-sized projects in the commercial domain, this switch to the short-term strategy has more or less already happened. However, national organisations seem to plan large software development projects which can stretch over *very* long periods and which need highly structured deliverables to maintain control. Up to now, all UK government system proposals are based on the use of SSADM as the working methodology and this is unlikely to change in the near future.

This should pose no real difficulty as this book is mainly geared to commercial organisations rather than governmental agencies. It has to be said that most of the examples of Chapter 3 and 'Crash' (see bibliography) are based on government projects which have consistently failed in a more or less spectacular fashion over the last thirty years. Most of these projects would have been developed using SSADM and, no doubt, this disaster-development paradigm is continuing (current examples: projects Swanwick, the air control centre that is only 3 years late – and counting; the LITS project, the RAF logistics exercise covered in Chapter 7; and the Read codes medical program). It will no doubt continue into the foreseeable future. However, for commercial organisations who need some sort of bottom-line effective solutions to meet serious corporate requirements, the strategies given in the section 'Modularity' and the next chapter should provide some useful inputs.

Summary: small is definitely beautiful and some suitable version of RAD is the only way to go.

Pilot scheme

In terms of risk minimisation, there is a great deal to be said for planning a pilot site run before scaling up to corporate-wide installation. (We are back to FoxMeyer of Texas again.)

The downside is fairly clear: a site has to be found; it will cost more to formally implement a pilot phase; it will add more time to the overall schedule; and the scaling performance is always something of an open question. ('Scaling' is defined as using a system under different circumstances from the given test environment, often using it in a much larger configuration or under heavier traffic conditions.)

But the advantages are overwhelming:

❑ Reduced size of project = reduced development work load;

❑ If the system is unworkable, then the risk is contained;

❑ Actual on-line operational performance can be evaluated;

❑ It provides a test vehicle for enhancements and upgrades.

This is all pretty much in line with the arch-guru of common sense, Fred Brooks, who had effectively delivered the last word on formal pilot systems in the middle 70s:

'Plan to throw one away - you will anyway' [9]

In other words, plan an initial pilot scheme and then go on to the scheduled mark 2 full-scale implementation. As a possible alternative, install a fully functioning system across the entire organisation (which, almost by definition, will not operate correctly). Then try to upgrade it with a rushed, hopefully-debugged, roughly-tested, fully-undocumented model. This to be implemented by some stressed-out design team working round the clock for weeks at a time. It is a choice.

As an encouragement to including a pilot scheme, let's see what can happen if you are the Foreign Office (FO) and don't plan to use a pilot... and your luck runs out.

> In 1987 the FO wanted to replace their obsolete accounting system and by 1988 their consultant had recommended a particular supplier to design the new system.

> In 1988, their problems were compounded when the existing system went down with no data backup. It made subsequent data comparisons between old and new somewhat suspect.

> February 1990 was not a good time for the FO. The system had been finally delivered about a year late. Within a few weeks of the delivery, the supplier went into liquidation. Shortly thereafter, the old system finally died, leaving the FO fully dependent on the new still 'buggy' software. This had now become the mother of all pilot-less systems and the resulting output data could not be trusted.

> 18 months later, the National Audit Office was still complaining that the installed system could not produce reliable figures and was uncertain as to its long term credibility [10, 11, 12].

Whether you are a drug company in Texas or the UK Government in London, it still makes a lot of sense to plan for a pilot scheme.

Modularity

From the previous section on RAD, it is clear that successful projects are potentially dependent on fast turnarounds. Small projects can be readily handled using standard prototyping techniques, but there is still the problem of the larger system requirements.

Objects

There is a means to resolve this issue, but there is a sting in the tail. It will entail using object-oriented programming techniques (Appendix 2). If you are very experienced, it enables you to develop finished applicable systems within weeks, sometimes even within days. And the sting?

❏ It may take years to get the management and workforce to that level of expertise and competency and could cost the organisation up to $100m in the process [13];

❏ It is not just the technology. There are the programming tools and test facilities which have to be acquired, installed and used by a workforce familiar with their capabilities and performance [14];

❏ There is the dramatic change of culture for developers, managers and quality control. In particular, the project management methods and priorities will have to be completely modified from the way SDLC projects were handled [15].

To summarise, do not be too surprised if the first few OO projects go disastrously wrong. Take it as normal and simply avoid using the learning process on mission-critical projects.

In effect, the whole company, from the executive down, has to invest heavily in the new approach before the benefits can become apparent. It is a great route but with a heavy price. However, there is one possible alternative way round the problems. It is called 'components'.

Components

Philosophically, this could be a very dramatic step forward for system development applications. At the most basic level, it offers the possibility of buying software functions and services off the peg. From, say, the supermarket down the road.

This is like trying to build a car in your home garage: you buy suspension units from one supplier, the fully assembled gearbox from another and the complete set of bodywork panels from a third source. And they all have the capability of working together with other bought-in units. No manufacturing required - just assembly.

Can this really work for software? Well, maybe. Let us assume that you want to add a text processor to a specific system. Under SDLC, you document the specification to the smallest detail, and then set out to design (and document and test and install) software to satisfy the required specification. Using OO technology, you define all the required parts as individual objects, and then program the code for each of these objects. Under a component strategy, you might possibly define all the basic elements of a text processor, *and then go out and buy each of these elements as pre-tested interactive programmed blocks.* The resulting saving in time is enormous, the associated risks drop dramatically, and the re-usability is virtually guaranteed [16].

The actual technical working of components across the network is a great deal more complex than that - involving more acronyms than bees at the honey pot. A simplified overview is given in Appendix 2. It sounds almost irresistible, but there are, as ever, some serious counter-indications:

❏ The whole approach depends on there being an agreed solid interface standard, and, as usual, there are currently two of them slugging it out - Microsoft's DCOM versus the Rest's CORBA;

❏ The market is still very new, exploding with start-up companies providing application consultancy, applying dedicated tools to generate the components and using specific commercial ORBs (Object Request Broker, the device which conforms to an interface standard [see above] and links components together);

❏ Once again, the culture of the organisation has to accept the component approach to system development and there will be a high learning curve at the management level.

For all that, the whole industry is awash with promises for tomorrow and significant work is being undertaken by system houses today [17]. Providing the standards issue can be contained, this still looks like the way system development will eventually have to go. The conceptual approach is too attractive to give up.

Iteration

Back to the world of common-sense. For a more effective system, be prepared to carry out the design more than once.

If you will recall, back in Chapter 4, it was stated that virtually every new design will constitute a brand-new approach because the technology had moved on so sharply in the two or three years since the last development exercise. And, from the section on 'evolution' at the start of this chapter, it was shown that dramatically new designs tend not to succeed. An evolutionary strategy, i.e. 'little and often', cuts across all these problem areas. (This is not the same function as the Brooks injunction 'to plan to throw one away'. In the current context, you plan to use the first, then use the replacement second, then use the replacement third.)

Real-life examples

First, let's see if 'second time round the block' really does improve matters. There are quite a number of actual projects out there where the second development phase, largely based on the poor results obtained from the first project, succeeded where the first one did not.

The London Ambulance Service

The London Ambulance Service (see the full discussion in Chapter 3). One of the often-quoted classic examples of project failure and mismanagement. To cover the ground again, briefly, the LAS system was intended to replace a paper and pencil transfer of information from a central controller to the ambulance crews with an innovative, high technology, low cost, computerised dispatch system. From inception in late 1990 to its demise in late 1992, it was a spectacular, if inevitable, catastrophe [18].

About two years later, another development programme was set in motion, this time with an appointed head of IT. The first step was to analyse the previous project and highlight the factors that had led to the debacle. In a nutshell, there was project hindsight. The next step was to handle the cultural and organisational problems. This was made dramatically easier precisely because the paymaster, in this case the government, knew *that the previous approach had led to disaster.* This means that the new project manager could negotiate with his masters: 'if you do not rethink your strategy, you know what will happen...' Suddenly, time-scales could be realistic, budgets made available on time, and so on. There was a client understanding of scope.

The second time round, with sound management and building on the lessons of the former project, the LAS dispatch system became pretty much a success in its field [19].

TAURUS

We can take a brief look again at Taurus (Transfer and AUtomated Registration of Uncertified Stock). It was the ultimate learning experience for the financial markets in London. For the cost of a mere £400 million (the overall figure varies but it is in this general band) and roughly 10 years work, the Stock Exchange learnt how not to implement, develop or manage an IT project - in this case a paperless share settlement system.

Once again, like the LAS, there was the huge leap forward, complex requirements, rigid timetables, ineffectual management - and, once again, a monumental bust in March 1993 about 2 years after the date when the system was first planned to be installed [20].

The Bank of England picked up the pieces and proposed a three year programme to provide an electronic share settlement service, to be called Crest, for a total cost of about £35 million. Once again, lessons were learnt, the overall objectives were slimmed down, and the end-users consulted for the minimum necessary features. In 1996 the system was installed. It was claimed to meet performance targets, on time and on budget. Whatever the truth, it was certainly considered good enough to be one of the three award winners for projects selected by the British Computer Society in 1997. The second-time-round team must have been doing something right [21].

Why is the second time round so much more effective that the first? All sorts of reasons will be given (see [19] again), but the prime reason is simply that it is the second time round. Familiarity brings its own reward.

Practical lessons

The above examples show that two full development cycles for a technically ambitious system will provide a good chance of project success. It is likely to be true, but the projected cost in time and effort would be totally unacceptable to any management team. (Although a look through the files will show that it does happen quite frequently, unacceptable or otherwise.) However, in line with the approach given in the section 'Evolution', what would happens if system changes were limited, the objectives strictly constrained, the methods conventional and the workforce and management familiar with the development tools and software? In other words, if the partnership is undertaken for a low-technology, limited deliverables system project. Under these circumstances the whole mechanics of the familiar project would be changed:

❑ The development team will be small;

❑ The previous experience and expertise will be of value;

❑ The test requirements will be severely reduced;

❑ Meetings and reviews will be drastically cut;

❑ Documentation requirements will be diminished;

❑ Time-to-deliver will be measured in months;

❑ Overall costs will probably be decimated.

All this, and a realistic chance that the system objectives would be achieved. Notice one other advantage. Having carried out the first system project in this way, the next low-cost low-timescale low-technology project (moving the system capability on by another small increment) will be familiar territory to the whole organisation. In effect, the strategy not only enables the current project to be carried out, it also prepares the development team and system client for success in future projects.

Keeping it simple enables you to do it again.

Summary

The basic model of a system is simple – just three connected elements: an input block, a converting process and an output block (Appendix 2). And yet, today, a software-based commercial system remains complicated, hard to capture and still very difficult to design and implement.

The practices discussed in this chapter will provide a sturdy framework for software system development, whatever the requirement. Most of the concepts have been established for the last few decades, but still do not get onto the strategic planning list. To recap the main points again:

❑   Keep system objectives modest rather than overly ambitious;

❑   Avoid standard methodologies based on SDLC;

❑   Always plan for a pilot installation;

❑   Use a fast-track coding strategy, i.e. objects or components;

❑   Expect to schedule a number of low-cost development cycles.

This approach can all be encapsulated with Figure 9.2 below (where the equivalent 'classical' system cost figure would be completely off the page).

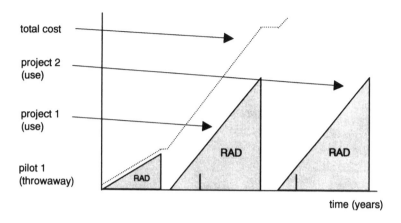

Figure 9.2   The development strategy

But note that this approach takes no account of the impact on the organisation and *that* is a specific problem that will have to be addressed in the next chapter.

References

1 Murphy J, SAP's drugs bust ends up in court, Computing, 24.9.1998, p.42
2 Glass R, Software Runaways, p.23, *(See under Bibliography)*
3 Collins T and Bicknell D, Crash, p.174, *(See under Bibliography)*
4 Christensen C, The Innovator's Dilemma, *(See under Bibliography)*
5 McConnell S, Rapid Development, *(See under Bibliography)*
6 Branton P, Has RAD lost its pace?, Computer Weekly, 5.6.1997, p.62
7 Avison D and Fitzgerald G, Information System Development: Methodologies, Techniques and Tools, p.17, McGraw Hill, 1995
8 Ker N, Small is beautiful, Computer Bulletin, April 1994, p.5
9 Brooks F, The mythical man month, p.116, *(See under Bibliography)*
10 Hughes C, Foreign Office computers 'lose' £50m, The Independent, 6.2.1991, p.4
11 Bevins A, Foreign Office's computer crisis, The Independent, 5.9.1991, p4
12 Government pledges not to repeat Foreign Office system errors, Computer Weekly, 14.11.1991, p.2

13 Freeman E, Is OO app dev worth the cost?, Datamation, March 97

14 Ruber P, Application Development: Today's Power Tools, Beyond Computing, March 1998

15 Fayad M and Laitinen M, Transition to Object-Oriented Software Development, p.14, *(See under Bibliography)*

16 Baer T, The culture of components, Application Development Trends, September 1998

17 Foley M, Objects for Business Apps are coming! But slowly, Datamation, May 1996

18 Smith S, The cost of living, Computer Weekly, 29.2.1996, p.36

19 999 Rescue, The Computer Bulletin, October 1997, p.22

20 Collins T and Bicknell D, Crash, p.174, *(See under Bibliography)*

21 Every one a winner, The Computer Bulletin, December 1997, p.19

Chapter 10 The new approach - people

Introduction

Information technology is ultimately about people. Those people who build new processors, design new applications, use software systems in their daily work, test and maintain the software and hardware packages, configure marketing and sales campaigns based on IT data, and manage global operations using IT-sourced instruments. IT, itself, is primarily a business tool which either succeeds or fails depending on how people apply it as an aid to meeting their overall commercial objectives. IT may run the shop but it is still people who run the IT - from the initial concept, through development, to the final, hopefully profitable, application within the organisation.

This chapter will take a fundamental look at the people behind the technological changes in the office. More particularly, it will look at the *roles* that need to exist in any successful organisation and the qualities required to meet those role functions. As we shall see, the impact of people is absolutely crucial, and the focus for this chapter is on how people and their characteristics will influence the success of new systems under development. The chapter breaks down naturally into two sections. The first comprises a brief review of the underlying concepts and needs associated with people working productively in any company, while the second will address the practical organisational requirements which will meet or satisfy these conceptual constraints

Underlying concepts

By now it should be clear – for any organisation, the prime strategic objective with regard to IT development is not necessarily the attainment of success, but is very definitely concerned with the prevention or minimisation of failure. It is true that success will be most welcome, but the absence of failure will, at least, enable the organisation to continue to survive. System development continues to be a high cost, high risk undertaking (again, see Chapters 2 and 3) and risk minimisation has to be high on the priority list. To understand the changes proposed in the second part of this chapter, four key areas will need to be explored at an abstract level:

❑ Culture;

❑ Control;

❑ Communication;

❑ Competence.

Culture

There are many professional definitions around, but, for our purposes, corporate culture can be loosely defined as 'the way the organisation runs'. It has two principal components – the attitudes and customs of the workforce and the leadership style of the senior management. In terms of laying out successful IT development programs, the senior management is the key factor. If the management style, professionalism, expectations and objectives of the corporate leaders are 'wrong', then the probability of project success sinks down through the floor.

> True-life department: the management of a higher education college made public one part of the new strategic objective – the development of an Access-based student database to be designed, tested and made available for use by the college administration. The specification? It should be completed within some 4 months.

Such a time-scale is indeed feasible. But note the lack of development objectives in terms of database format, number of anticipated records, performance criteria, quality aspects, built-in safety features, interaction with other management systems, and so on and so on. Just the simple delivery date.

This is an example of a project demanding to fail. It strongly suggests that the senior management has no idea what is involved in an effective and successful IT project implementation. Or what is wanted from such an exercise. In this case, the culture is wrong and all that can be done is to apply appropriate personal survival techniques [1].

Another view of cultural mis-match. Some industries have an approach that generally prevents or inhibits the leadership from supplying competent management-support to an IT project. Any area of activity, where orders are issued in the confident expectation that they will be rigidly obeyed without question, is unlikely to be a suitable candidate for successful IT development. We are talking about authority without accountability. This will potentially apply to the military services, could well apply to some civil service operations such as prison or security organisations, and will almost certainly apply to any commercial or political operation where the culture is essentially authoritarian. The basic problem is that such organisations demand adherence to a pre-determined set of rules rather than any display of management skill or potential leadership qualities from the senior staff. In other words, they do not handle a crisis on its merits, but apply culturally 'correct' procedures. For a clear and comprehensive review of this problem and its underlying sources, Dixon's book on military incompetence remains illuminating – in particular see Chapter 22 onwards [2].

Why does a mainly dictatorial management provide such difficulties? Because, as a broad simplistic generalisation, such management tends *not* to be flexible, capable of learning, adaptive, or necessarily competent in management. Which is fine for dictatorships, but these are precisely the values needed for strategic leadership of IT projects.

> Examples: The UK Ministry of Defence has a strong track record in funding IT system projects. It has a less enviable record in the successful implementation of such projects. (See, for example, the CHOTS report in Chapter 3.) Throughout the early 90s it was regularly criticised by the National Audit Office for repeating the errors of the previous period despite assurances that improvements would be implemented [3]. In the mid 90s, another critical NAO report found that 90% of defence projects were failing to meet original deadlines [4].

In summary, before setting out any serious program of organisational change, address the manangement on the the following issues:

❏ Ensure that the senior management understand the main problem areas of IT development and the need for 'sympathetic' leadership;

❏ Ensure that they recognise the need for ongoing management support (for 'support' read 'funding') during the development activity;

❏ Ensure that they have generated a realistic and well-defined set of objectives for the new system.

Control

The following paragraphs are specifically addressed to the Managing Director, or the Chief Executive Officer, or the relevant VP, or whoever is responsible for running the big show.

To date, there has been one important if unspoken question, and it has been sliding through the previous chapters like a tapeworm through the gut:

What exactly were you doing while the project was going belly-up?

If the application of IT is a strategic matter (and anything that causes losses of fifty billion dollars per year in the United States is likely to be strategic), and if over 80% of IT developments regularly fail (Chapter 2), then the Chief Executives or Directors are probably not doing enough. To address failure minimisation properly, this will surely have to change.

What is the current situation? For most development programs, there are three principle interacting roles: development, project, and client, as shown in Figure 10.1.

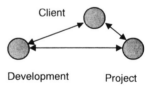

Figure 10.1 The key roles

Development This can comprise an outside group, internal department, single team, or a stand-alone design engineer. In any case, this is where system design, software design, test and documentation activities are carried out.

Project The project manager, or team, seeks to monitor the status of the development project, establish what progress – or lack thereof – has been achieved over the last given period, negotiate realistic new delivery dates, and report crucial project information or problem areas up to the senior management for their attention.

Client This consists of project paymasters, the management who will involve themselves with the application of the new system, and the actual end users who will be operating the system data screens.

In order to get the senior management staff more active in IT development, we are going to have to add an extra dimension to the above diagram. This will introduce the concept of 'control', i.e. the function properly carried out by the chief executive or equivalent, and this is illustrated in Figure 10.2. In turn, this raises the issue of how competently the senior management can influence the IT programs. How to address and resolve this issue within the corporate structure will be discussed in the next main section of the chapter.

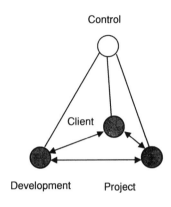

Figure 10.2 The new structure

Communications

In any area of group activity, communication between group members becomes a key factor in the success of the endeavour. And when developer and client make serious claims against each other, then communications must have been the first casualty in the relationship.

> A brief review of the LITS project (Chapter 7) shows just what can happen when inter-group communications breaks down. In this case, over a period of time the client of an important strategic project (the Royal Air Force) suffered an almost total loss of trust and confidence in the selected development authority (IBM) [5]. Once this occurred, the real facts or the actual events hardly mattered.

Communications comes in all shapes and sizes from the body language seen across a restaurant table to the latest e-mailed minutes of a government committee meeting. Certainly, communication is the activity that takes up most of the managers time and is probably the most important of his or her undertakings [6]. For a project to succeed, it should be obvious that there must be clear and unrestricted links from all members of the group to all other members of the group and those links must be gainfully employed. How can this basic model go wrong?

At its simplest level, communications is all about the intent to provide a data transfer - some sort of message - between two or more individuals or interactive units. Party A speaks or signals in some way (semaphore, message slip, satellite link, whatever) and this is detected and understood by party B. But it does not always work properly and there are many ways in which this model can be degraded into imperfect or non-communication [7]. This can be simply illustrated as shown in Figure 10.3 below:

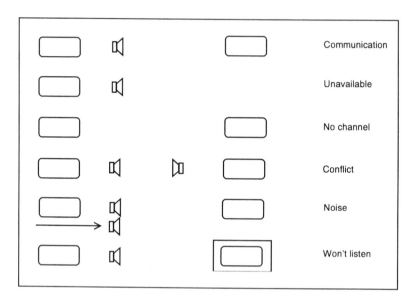

Figure 10.3 Communication models

Working down Figure 10.3 we can see the following possibilities:

❑ Top line - A talks through the loudspeaker and B is ready to listen - the perfect case for communication;

❑ B is unavailable - on holiday, at another meeting, or thinking of some other more interesting topic while looking attentive;

❑ There is no transfer media. Perhaps all messages out of the department have to be sent with the prior approval of your boss, and he is off visiting other sites;

❏ B is not in a listening mood, since he has a message of his own which he thinks is vastly more important;

❏ B is trying to listen, but there are other inputs masking your message and B cannot make out what you are saying through the resulting noise;

❏ B has already made up his mind and is not going to listen whatever you have to say ('don't confuse me with facts').

These problem areas can (and do) regularly occur between individuals, departmental/divisional/global corporate entities, and one or more inter-trading companies. When any of the above problems occur, it is necessary to detect, identify and address the source problem with some urgency.

Competence

Consider the local or national baseball or football team. It carries out the group-related activity and needs the best possible team it can muster. This is achieved via two possible routes: cheap or expensive. On the one hand, young players are judged to have potential and are brought in for subsequent buffing and polishing over time. On the other, proven experts are acquired for immediate injection into the team's activities. Either way, ongoing training will continue to hone the capability of this group to the maximum.

Why seek to achieve the best performance from the team? There is only one real reason – competition. There are other units out there carrying on the same activities as you and, like you, they want to *win*. With that scenario in place, only the best may be good enough.

Back to your organisation. Independent of the nature of your business, if you can create a competitive edge in your administration by reducing costs or providing a better service compared to your rivals, this will generate a significant strategic advantage in the marketplace. One recognised way to achieve this edge is to develop and install more effective IT systems than your competitors. And the better systems are nearly always developed by the more professional and more experienced work groups. Hence the strategic need for top quality system development teams [8].

Summary

The last few pages have discussed the framework defining the expertise and corporate structure needed in an organisation intending to develop (or cause to be developed) successful software systems. All the areas discussed are generic and all of them are certainly strategic. Note that if these areas have been successfully addressed then the *climate* for ongoing change and enhancement in other areas will have become well established. In particular recall the need for:

❏ A corporate culture sympathetic to IT system development needs. This could include a fast decision turnaround process and a sympathetic understanding of changing environment pressures;

❏ A control and overview mechanism enabling senior management to monitor and guide the development and project teams;

❏ Operational and effective communication chains active between all interested parties;

❏ Highly trained, skilled and motivated development staff.

The real challenge comes in trying to provide a practical organisational environment that can meet or satisfy all the above requirements.

The organisation for system development

This section will set out to establish and define all the staff functions that should be introduced into the client or 'receiver' organisation. If implemented, they will ultimately enable system development activities to be undertaken in an effective, secure, and controlled manner. These staff functions are not particularly novel, but they do still seem to be needed.

Assumptions

❏ The development roles outlined in Figure 10.1 will already be present.

❏ The new roles will be needed independent of whether the organisation is purely a 'client' or has an internal 'developer' function.

❏ The underlying strategic objective is to minimise the risk or impact of development failure.

❏ The roles may be carried out by a whole department or be a part of one person's workload. It is the presence of the role, not its implementation, that is important.

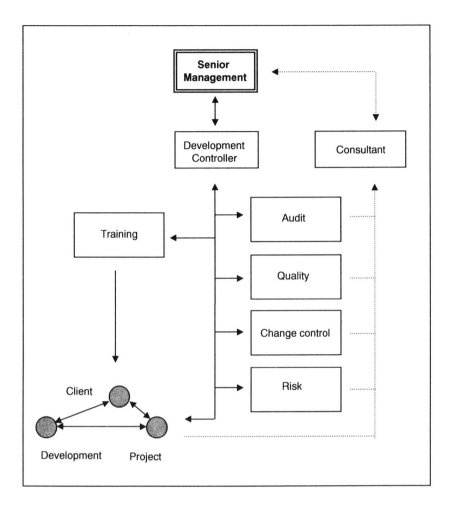

Figure 10.4. The new organisational structure

Senior management

Figure 10.4 lays out the proposed structure of the organisation. We will analyse it top-down and start with the senior management – the generic term for whoever is in charge of the organisation. And therein lies the problem. Whoever is running the company is likely to know a great deal about oranges, coffins or gold futures, or whatever the trading area of interest. But, he or she is unlikely to know very much about Information Technology or system development because it is outside their specific area of commercial interest. In addition, IT is technical, complicated and dramatically changing every year or so. Nevertheless, system development, installation, and application is an important strategic activity since it is expensive, used globally in every department and on every corporate site, and can dramatically affect the competitive status of the company [9]. As shown in Chapter 3 and elsewhere, over-ambitious targets or inadequate control of system development can virtually destroy almost any organisation. Once it is seen as a strategic subject, it is clear that the senior management will have to handle IT in a responsible and capable manner, whether they understand it or not [10].

One possible solution to the problem is to appoint a CIO (Chief Information Officer) or an IT Director who will be responsible for all IT related matters – in Figure 10.4 given the somewhat bland title of 'Development Controller'. But for senior management to depend on this controller may still prove problematic as we shall see in the following paragraphs.

Development controller

As suggested above, this is a reasonably senior position with overall responsibility for all aspects of the development program. One person has to be the focal point of the project and this is it. Clearly, it is a challenging job. He or she has to motivate the staff, co-ordinate many different work strands, resolve priorities, handle a variety of disputes related to different engineering disciplines, successfully scan an enormous amount of data on a daily basis, and liaise with bosses who do not always understand the engineering complexities of a given problem. In effect, he or she runs the project and communicates with senior management.

And this is where the problem creeps in. The development controller has direct line responsibility, i.e. has a vested interest in the success of the project. The controller's own career prospects will almost certainly be affected by the success or failure of the development program. Under these circumstances, in reporting 'upwards', there is an understandable tendency to put the most positive slant on progress reports, problem resolution, test results, documentation deliveries and budgetry uncertainties. Under enough pressure, schedules may be shaved (or butchered, if the problems are serious enough), deliveries may be reduced, test strategies thinned down, and so on. The controller is only human in a sometimes difficult world. The most extreme example of this could be the commercial pressures related to the maintenance of a public-utility nuclear power plant. A fictional view of this role has been given by the entertainment world [11], but a more chilling example lay with the actual events of Three Mile Island in 1979 [12].

Consultant

This is where the consultant steps in. The summary of the situation is straightforward:

❏ The senior management does not always understand the technicalities of IT related applications;

❏ Nevertheless, in order to make strategic decisions, the senior management needs an expert view of the IT development activities;

❏ That view should be unbiased and independent and will be best provided by someone with no direct vested interests.

An external consultant with suitable system experience will satisfy all these criteria. It is a high cost per unit-time solution, but he or she will only be needed intermittently – say possibly for 2 days three times a year. Such an individual can probe into all areas of the program and can provide expert and impartial reports on demand. It is a risk – you have to find the right person and not all consultants are competent – but the odds are a lot shorter than the alternative solutions.

Audit

This is the first of the technical management roles shown in Figure 10.4. The idea behind it is simple: to detect a problem in the current development program *before the problem has become a crisis.* This is equivalent to, say, the warning lights on the car dashboard. If the oil warning light comes on, it does not mean that there is no oil, but it does suggest that oil should be added to the engine (motor) in the near future. Similarly, audits can have a preventative function.

There are in fact two primary functions for audits: historic and current – and, despite the fact that they are not usually applied, both of them are vital. They provide the only on-line diagnostic tool to the development project with a reasonably fast reporting capability.

Historic audits

This seeks to answer two important questions related to the last project: a) what went wrong; and b) how much did it cost while going wrong.

a) You can see that all this raking up of mistakes and errors must be as popular as hair-lice to the project team involved. On the other hand, the only possible justification for a total disaster is that it is an opportunity to learn how not to do it again. A lack of audits leads inevitably to no learning and to continuing the disaster regime (we are back to Chapter 2 again).

b) The whole question of cost over-runs has bedevilled the software industry for the last thirty years. And there is very little feedback available on the actual, as opposed to the proposed, costs for any project. As discussed in Chapter 6, a feasibility study is carried out for a new system, cost projections are generated and a budget prepared. The perceived benefit is configured into the equation and a clear profit is established (hereinafter called the 'Business Plan'). At this point, the company signs on for, say, $30 million of new system development. And then reality takes over. Again, no-one wants to take a chainsaw to yesterday's dreams, but the learning curve on costs has got to start somewhere.

Current audits

The early warning instrument for systems under development. Regular status check-ups, say, every month or other month will potentially identify problems as they occur, allowing corrective action to be undertaken. Given the current patterns of success for modern system design (Chapter 2 again), deviation from the expected is virtually guaranteed to happen – it is only the specific direction that the problem takes that is uncertain. But, regardless of their utility, external audits of ongoing work are not necessarily a popular idea with the managers under audit:

> Quebec Bridge was being built in the 1900s under the leadership of the consulting engineer Theodore Cooper. He had unilaterally extended the original specification of the bridge without providing any additional strengthening or support. A proposal for an independent audit in 1903 was angrily rejected. As a compromise, he was prepared to appoint his own candidate to be the auditor. In 1906, the extra steel added to the bridge far outweighed the original estimate, but Cooper ensured that this was ignored. In 1907 the bridge started to buckle under the added weight. It finally collapsed that August with the loss of 75 workmen [13].

For all the problems, an audit function will provide powerful trend information and early warning indicators to the development controller [14]. But there is a sting in the tail. The audit role has to be carried out professionally. Any indication that short-cuts were taken, or that insufficient attention was given to rooting out problems – and retribution shall surely follow [15].

Quality

Assuming it ever gets installed, the operability and reliability of the system will have a crucial impact on the satisfaction level of the client. These criteria are the concerns of the Quality Manager. He or she has two important functions: a) to ensure that the system is designed to be maintainable – Quality Assurance; and b) to keep the system in a maintainable condition after installation – Quality Control.

Quality Assurance

The best system results occur when the quality is built in with the design and planned for at the outset. What is certain is that quality cannot be added after the design has been completed. It will involve some or all of the following:

Software   For a good maintenance capability, the software should be well structured (i.e. built in modules). The software should also have a well defined test strategy.

Programming   Large programs can be analysed for underlying structure and programming violations. But this can prove an expensive option.

System test   For full system tests, there are other software tools which can reduce the long term failure rate. However, they are also expensive and would probably only be used for space equipment or nuclear installations.

Documentation A comprehensive set of structured system documents – defined, written, signed off and stored.

Quality Control

To set up a good quality control environment for installed operational systems, the following issues should be addressed:

Strategy   A corporate strategy plan for quality must be proposed, accepted and implemented. Quality can only operate on a defined top-down basis;

Formal design   The use of structured development techniques will ensure that agreed and tested products and accepted documents will be delivered to the end-user. The program code will be well documented and will conform to good design practice;

Archive   The ongoing maintenance support for the system will depend on the ready availability of the system documentation at the time of the maintenance activity. To ensure this, an archive, perhaps on and off-site, will need to be set up to include specifications, code, test criteria and related results;

CM   Configuration Management is concerned with the identification of every part in the system, every version, upgrade and variant of that part, and the documentation that covers each version, upgrade and variant. CM requires an archive for documentation storage and is another part of the framework that will enable maintenance to be effective.

Poor quality adds to the defect rate in software code, to overall schedule slippage, to increased maintenance costs, and to client dissatisfaction. It is simply not worth it. Learn about quality and then apply it [16, 17].

Change control

Depending on the source, change can be a force for good or for bad. The ability to create and inject change, i.e. new products or innovative processes, into the market place gives a strong competitive advantage for any trading organisation. Conversely, external changes, such as a new user requirement, introduced halfway through a test cycle constitute a most unwelcome threat to the new system (Chapter 5). This latter form of change can cause almost continuous design modification and endemic project instability.

Change analysis

Changes which can adversely affect development projects tend to come in three major flavours, as shown in Figure 10.5, and these largely depend on the state of the project.

Phase I   Feature creep (usually requested by the client). As the client
                        learns more about the art of the possible, so extra 'bells and
                        whistles' are added to the original specifications.

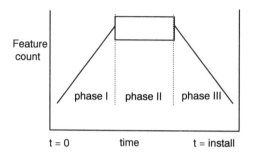

Figure 10.5   Project change

Phase II   The middle phase is where any number of unplanned,
                        uncontrolled external inputs occur. These will alter the rules
                        of the game – for better or worse. They can vary from a
                        corporate buy-out, to a chief engineer's pregnancy, to a
                        change of national tax structure. The most likely is for all
                        three to occur in the same timeframe.

Phase III   Feature cuts (usually generated by the developer). This is the
                        phase where the time-to-deliver date takes on an almost
                        mystical significance and the knives are out should anyone
                        seek to challenge it. A set of bad test results tends to
                        eliminate all further testing, and the lack of one document
                        may lead to the scrapping of the entire documentation plan.

It should be obvious that these are stereotyped examples, and they
represent the typical changes that can be met. Most of them will radically
affect the project schedules, going back to the earliest stage in order to
rewrite the product specification such as to incorporate the change (and then
redesign the basic logical model, and then re-code – and so on)

Change limitation

The trick is to get everything right at the feasibility stage. In reality this is
unlikely, but any later corrective action should require formal approval from

the change review board (or equivalent). This review board, run by the 'change co-ordinator', will have been set up at the start of the project with defined membership, approval procedures, boundaries of influence, change-notification lists and reporting structures. It will try to contain the number of proposed modifications to the requirements, but it is ultimately a question of good judgement: trading added cost or schedule constraint against priority or need.

Consider the air traffic control improvement program (known as the AAS or Advanced Automation System) of the FAA, Federal Aviation Administration. It was to be a state-of-the-art computerised break-though in technology.

1981 New AAS program announced.

1983 Operational target, 1991. Cost \$2.5 billion. New software language Ada.

1988 Cost projections rose to \$4.3 billion as IBM won the development contract after a *4 year* design competition with Hughes (the competition itself cost \$1 billion).

1992 IBM working on the final (9th) revision of the master software suite ISSS (Initial Sector Suite System).

1993 FAA agreed to (re)finalise the requirements for the ISSS. A comprehensive review of the project was ordered (the first independent project audit) following an added cost exposure of \$1.2 billion for modifying existing requirements.

1994 New total cost estimates rose to \$7.3 billion. New development team specified. New ISSS specification agreed. The old project (and a few billion dollars) was then cancelled.

1995 New development partner assigned with new reduced system targets.

The initial objectives, especially for the system software, were over-ambitious and the requirements never seemed to stabilise over the life of the project. Within this framework, the result was inevitable [18, 19, 20].

The best approach is to spend more time at the front end getting the specifications right and then to limit subsequent changes. This is not generally popular with the client management or the developer work teams, and the probabilities are not on your side. But things can go terribly wrong any other way.

Risk

At one level, it is almost pure gambling. You invest some time and effort now in the expectation of maybe saving considerable aggravation and cost at some undefined time in the future. Perhaps a more polite word would be 'insurance'. Whatever, risk management is generally a worthwhile activity since everyone wins – whoever addresses the problem of risk in a project will almost certainly enjoy a better outcome than those who consistently refuse to address it [21].

Close members of the family are 'contingency planning and 'crisis management'. For example, in the last years of the 90s, millions of dollars were spent globally on examining every possible impact of the millennium bug in and out of the organisation. In addition, everyone evaluated solutions and work-rounds to the perceived danger. At a more prosaic level, most people invest in floppy disks or more exotic media and take back-ups of their software on a regular basis to minimise the potential impact of the hard disk malfunctioning.

For any project risk there are two types of probability of occurrence: low and high; and there are two types of project impact: low and high. This is illustrated in Figure 10.6. The bottom line is that only the high impact types of risk need be pursued, i.e. all the right-hand areas. Risks falling into this region require some sort of fallback solution to be established.

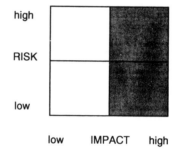

Figure 10.6 The risk square

Professional risk management calls up three separate activities: risk identification, risk evaluation and subsequent risk minimisation. To be effective, the position calls for experience and judgement since potential breakdowns or disasters are being looked for in a system that has yet to be built. At the same time, risk containment costs money and there has to be a clear perception of value. Earthquake insurance for a site in the Thames basin is likely to be a somewhat ineffective exercise, whereas, for a location on the San Andreas fault...

Classic example:

❑ Identification: loss of mains power to the entire plant;.

❑ Evaluation: probability low; impact high; possible data loss if power is suddenly removed; loss of operation if power removed for an extended period of time;

❑ Minimisation: add UPS (Uninterruptible Power Supply).

The real question in this relatively trivial case is: does the added cost of the UPS – which may be thousands of pounds or euros, etc. – provide peace of mind against the relatively low risk of loss of power. That is something the risk manager has to propose and for the senior management to approve, or disapprove on a per-case basis.

Each project should end up with a whole database full of identified risks (and fallback solutions) and these will have be tracked through the life of the project. Looking back over the initial conditions of the FAA project above, it should be clear that effective risk management at the outset could well have saved hundreds of millions of dollars.

Training

Slowly, training is becoming recognised as one of the more important activities in the project world. It has three principal features:

❑ It provides time to implement strategic modifications;

❑ It keeps the staff up to date with the new technologies;

❑ It is a vehicle for putting across the (new) corporate culture.

Time

There is a paradox which is still bubbling over from the last chapter. At one point we say: 'evolve, move slowly and simply, do not change anything dramatically', while at another point, 'switch now from the standard life cycle or SSADM methodology and immediately embrace, say, RAD with objects.' The way to square this circle, to get these two opposed concepts to embrace is through the mechanism of training.

Let us take the C++ software language as an example. It could equally have been Java, or SQL but C++ will do. Now let's look at the key problem area – the time it takes to become proficient in this language. Well, it all depends on what you mean by 'proficient'.

❏ A standard course will take about 4 days. At the end of that time, you will be able to carry out simple basic instructions and coding.

❏ In the first 3 to 6 months, and under the tutelage of a C++ master, you will be able to put together some fairly rough lines of code which will, nevertheless, sometimes work as required. When something goes wrong you will still need a lot of support.

❏ Over the next one to two years, you will start to provide quality-enhanced packages containing lines of code with good commenting, error detecting, and full test capabilities. Elegant design and independence are starting to appear.

❏ After about three years you will be competent to teach the next generation (and, in turn, despair of their potential).

This training program may be long enough but is not in the same scale as that necessary to certify a professional accountant, surgeon, or pilot. (Perhaps that is why software failure rates are way above those of plane crashes or post-operational mortality.)

Back to the project. Any strategic change of direction, say, moving from one methodology to another, or changing the software operating system, will take about two years to be fully absorbed by the all the different workforces and their related disciplines. And this is about the same time needed to provide competence for the workforce in the new technology. Training and its delaying action provides the time to get the change in strategy fully installed in the organisation.

Technology

Training is not just about the first four days. To be effective, it should be a planned program of graded courses run from the Human Resource (HR) department. But not everyone is allowed the time.

> In one class on basic SQL, one trainee came up to me in some distress. Her organisation had asked her to begin the design of a new very large relational database in the next 6 months and she had to get some DBA (DataBase Administrator) experience. But you are now only just learning the rudiments of SQL. Yes, that may be, but my project is still starting up in 6 months time.

Competence is such a precious strategic commodity, it seems a pity for companies to ignore it.

Culture

Let's go back to the FAA project again. By 1992, give or take a year or so, morale was at an absolute nadir and moving smartly downwards. This could be considered the Nobel Prize-winning death-march and the workforce knew it. One approach could have been to institute a set of training courses to be given to the entire workforce. Not about technology or management technique, but this time simply putting the strategic message across that everyone should know, say, that there was now a line drawn in the sand, that they were all part of the team and there was a new set of defined goals. (Of course, if there was no new strategic message to deliver then nothing would help, but that is another problem.)

As an overview, training is a powerful tool that can be used to to tune the competence and morale of the workforce. In this context, it is worth recalling that the workforce is the only real vehicle you have got to develop systems which can achieve the desired strategic objectives.

Summary

This chapter has been a review of people filling appropriate roles in a development project. At the same time, it has also been a fundamental investigation into reducing the possibility of failure while developing systems. There were a number of performance criteria established and 3 main mechanisms will be involved in addressing these criteria:

❑ Any organisation with development ambitions has to address the following factors: culture, control, communications and competence;

❑ Error minimisation will use project control techniques such as change control, risk management and quality procedures (see Figure 10.4);

❑ Output monitoring will detect potential failure-inducing signals using multiple feedback loops. These feedback loops are standard in engineering control mechanisms [22], and the proposals discussed in this chapter provide three independent feedback paths which are illustrated in the system view given in Figure 10.7.

- The Project Management liaises directly with the development and client teams and inputs all major decisions and project milestones to the Development Controller, say, once a week.

- The independent Audit Controller probes the overall development progress and reports his or her results to the Development Controller, say, once every six to eight weeks.

- The Consultant reports on status directly to Senior Management, say, every six to eight months.

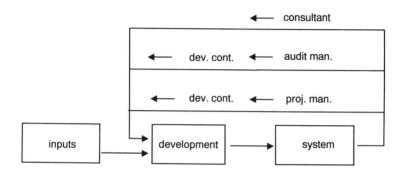

Figure 10.7 The feedback paths

Finally, it is worth noting that there are number of new positions discussed here and funding them will definitely add to the overall development budget. On the other hand, these added costs pale into insignificance compared to the failure of a mission-critical project.

References

1 Yourdon E, Death March, *(See under Bibliography)*

2 Dixon N, On the Psychology of Military Incompetence, *(See under Bibliography)*

3 Ward M, MoD criticised for repeated errors on major IT projects, Computing, 27.10.1994, p.3

4 Moules J, MoD fears costly delays in project procurement, Computing, 1.6.1995, p.2

5 Collins T, RAF chief to the rescue, Computer Weekly, 11.12.1997, p.20

6 Baron R, Behaviour in Organisations, Chapter 10, Allyn and Bacon, 1986

7 Bronzite M, Developing Information Systems – The Managers Guide, Chapter 8, Addison Wesley, 1991

 8 Webster B, The Real Software Crisis, Byte Magazine, January 1996

 9 Earl M, Management Strategies for Information Technology, p.2, Prentice Hall, 1989

10 Bowen D, Terminal Failures, Independent on Sunday (Business Supplement, p.1), 3.12.1995

11 Firm director Bridges J, The China Syndrome, 1979

12 Bignall V and Fortune V, Understanding Systems Failures, p.25, *(See under Bibliography)*

13 Collins T, Pushing projects beyond their limits, Computer Weekly, 26.11.1998, p.74

14 Bentley D, Applying the brakes on runaway projects, Computer Weekly, 9.6.1994, p.28

15 Bruce R and Ashworth J, Coopers faces record fine for Maxwell audit failures, The Times, 2.2.1999, p.25

16 McConnell S, Rapid Development, p.69, *(See under Bibliography)*

17 DeJesus E, State of the Art – Control Quality, Byte Magazine, September 1996, p.82

18 Glass R, Software Runaways, p.56, *(See under Bibliography)*

19 Hinson orders review of Advanced Automation System, Airport Report Express, 15.12.1993

20 FAA replaces AAS management team, Airport Report Express, 7.3.1994

21 Keen J, ROI – The risk of positive thinking, Datamation, September 1998

22 Vowler J, A feast for developers, Computer Weekly, 5.119.95, p.14

Fundamentals

We have finally arrived at the true centre of things. This is where the owner of the black leather chair subtly operates the levers of power, where decisions are made which directly impact the continued good health of the entire organisation. To make things absolutely clear, we are talking about the 'Senior Management' block shown in Figure 11.1. The various titles of such a role are shown on the left-hand side while the principal functions are indicated on the right.

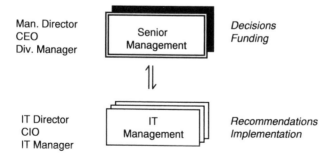

Figure 11.1 Function

If you will recall, part of the title of this book is 'A Strategic Framework'. Well, this is the chapter where we get to review some key aspects of strategic management as applied to the IT application arena.

Accountability

Just to set the right climate for what follows, we can now resolve one of the issues that may have been nagging you since the beginning of the book: who carries the ultimate responsibility for IT projects? Answer: it can only be the senior management since these are the only people who control budgets, who can sign off and who can shut down projects. They may take advice, but the decision-making and funding allocation is still all theirs – and has to be all theirs. Whatever good graces or misfortunes await the project, the members of the executive must finally carry responsibility for the outcome. From a strategic viewpoint, therefore, perhaps the most important issue in the entire field of software system development is the effectiveness of the non-IT corporate leaders. To underline it again, they are the only ones to control every facet of the Information Technology cost, development, quality, maintainability, and application in the organisation. So, with all humility, we shall seek here to design an optimum senior executive for IT system purposes. And to define the leadership qualities and style that will minimise the possibility of system development failure. It must surely be the most business-critical exercise in the whole book.

Scope

This chapter will contain a whole raft of lists, proposals, qualities, and requirements specifically related to the performance of senior management. The truth is – taking on the whole lot at once may simply end up causing severe corporate indigestion. So it may be more reasonable to break up the total task into a number of phases, and initially address just one or two of the proposals that make particular sense in your organisation. Anyway, let's start with the general limits and boundaries relating to this analysis of senior management.

Commercial objective

There is only one basic goal in any commercial environment: corporate survival. If the organisation, division, trading unit, whatever, is still in existence, say, a number of years after taking office, then the management must be doing something right [1]. The rest is largely detail.

Style

Whether you are driven by an over-riding need to succeed, or you are a caring supportive parental figure, or, again, an unfeeling machine with a central processor for a heart – the only real matter was addressed in the previous section, i.e. is the organisation surviving or not. The simple truth is that 'management style', *per se,* is not all that important. If a good rapport with the workforce helps you, so be it. On the other hand, if you have to implement a business process re-engineering plan, then substantial numbers of staff may well suffer being 'downsized' [2, 3]. The ship must not sink: but how you achieve that is, perhaps, up to you.

IT

Information technology and related applications constitute one of the more important strategic weapons in the arsenal of any organisation. It is strategic because the cost of using it takes up a significant proportion of corporate funds; the impact of getting it wrong is likely to be catastrophic; it is of global application in all departments and company sites; and strategic corporate decisions are heavily dependent on the use of IT generated data. It follows that IT itself must be treated strategically [4].

General management

This chapter will not concern itself with the general properties of management. While qualities such as corporate leadership, drive, boardroom charisma, *et al,* are fascinating – there are plenty of other better-qualified sources available to discuss these issues.

Computing

The actual nuts-and-bolts details of system development and project management are also not relevant here. Leave that to the Data Manager, IT director, or CIO.

Business climate

It is assumed that the trading position of the company is, at least, adequate and that the internal politics are no worse than usual. The time to sort out strategic arrangements is when things are going reasonably well. A collapsing market or the arrival of a potentially terminal lawsuit is no time to address long-term planning.

Key elements of the environment

This chapter will review the crucial setting in which development work can be carried out. This is something that only senior management have the responsibility and power to address. One view of the overall requirement is given in Figure 11.2 where all the building blocks are assembled to create a reasonably stable development environment.

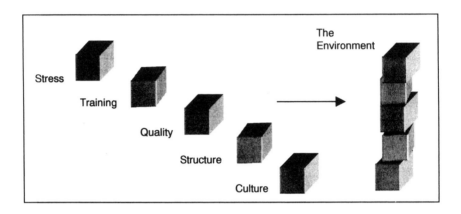

Figure 11.2 The environment building blocks

Culture

The truth is – if you get this section right, the rest tends to follow. It is the foundation on which all other business activities will be built. Conversely, it is also the one element that is most difficult to change. Modifying inappropriate values is like changing the course of a supertanker – it takes a reasonably sustained effort and the results may be painfully slow.

Think small

System projects are best served by taking small bites at the cherry, or at least the successful ones are (see Chapter 9). It is always tempting to go for the total business integration, the new enterprise-wide philosophy, or switch to the latest all-singing development tool. If this book has only one message, it has to be that going for the big one usually proves to be a very traumatic experience.

Workforce

At the beginning of the new millennium, the inter-relationship between the organisation and its IT related workforce is still undergoing dramatic changes. The projections and impacts of 'Future Shock' from two decades ago are slowly working their way through to business and industrial centres [5]. As usual, there is no right or wrong approach, but some of the following methods of employment may repay further consideration.

Once, in the good old days, there was only one type of employee: the permanently employed who had a job for life unless dismissed, relocated or pensioned-off. Today they are still there in diminishing numbers, but now they may be working alongside others. These will possibly include some key staff equipped, connected and working from home, i.e. teleworking [6]. There will also be the temporarily employed (say, a 1 year contract, renewable). Another buzzword interchangeable with Facility Management (FM) is 'outsourcing'. This is the devolving to outside parties of full responsibility for implementing non-core activities in your organisation. Examples could be: transport; training; or even the entire IT operations. It is tempting, but there are, as usual, a number of serious pitfalls [7, 8]. Other alternatives include the job-share (two people carrying out one job function), the freelance part-timer, the contractor (specific development skills, hired from an agency), an external team (a group employed to undertake just one specific task in the project), interim management [9] and the strategic consultant. It could all be a rich mine of expertise and talent, or a catastrophic clash of ideas, priorities and personalities. And you have to fix the mix.

Time management

This section relates to the organisation's attitude to planning and schedules. There are still some commercial organisations around trying to develop systems where the technical assessment of 'time required to develop system', say 24 months, is automatically reduced by the marketing or sales teams to a lower value, say 18 months. This, it is hoped, will improve the competitive status of the bid [10, 11]. (To be fair, with some clients, this seems to be an accepted practice. First you bid to get the job, and then, some time later, you re-negotiate to get a realistic, more extended schedule along with a fair price for the increased workload. There are examples in Chapter 3). However, where the development team is encouraged to work to the reduced timescale, only disaster can and usually does result:

❑ Stress levels on the personnel will only induce added errors;

❑ Reduced timescales will call for serious corner-cutting;

❑ Test activity will have to be severely reduced;

❑ 'Bad-news' reporting will be suppressed;

❑ Pre-delivery team morale will sink through the floor;

❑ Post-delivery maintenance costs will go through the roof.

In the long run, it is cheaper, far cheaper, to carry out a *timely* development, that is, where the job is realistically budgeted, staffed and scheduled for a well designed, well documented, well tested, well installed output generating a well satisfied client. However, for this to occur, such a development regime will need the full, public, and sustained support of senior management.

IT leadership

The key attributes required are outlined in Figure 11.3 where one specific quality, in effect, drives the rest :

Competence

This may be vague and difficult to define, but, for all that, it is absolutely crucial for the effective management and control of IT related activities. There have been reports of poor interaction between the chief executive of a company and the IT department. What contact does exist is often based on FUD (fear, uncertainty and doubt). In one survey, commissioned for The Guardian newspaper of London, over 40% of the IT professionals said they felt that their non-IT managers did not understand their work [12]. This constitutes a significant, if slightly worrying, input. Let's restate the problem logically:

❑ All strategic items need support from senior management (SM);

❑ Information technology is a strategic item;

❏ Some SM do not understand IT or its strategic importance;

❏ What is not understood cannot be properly supported or assessed.

In short, the SM should have a top-level knowledge of all the strategic elements of their business, *including* information technology. Only then can the executive operate effectively in making operational judgements and decisions. (We will return to this topic under 'Training'.) While on the subject, it should be obvious that the corporate decision-making responsibility cannot be delegated to the IT manager or director. The IT representative has the given role of advising, preparing recommendations, and implementing the board's requirements. But he or she is not answerable to the shareholders; will not have to judge what is best for the overall organisation; is not allowed anywhere near strategic decision-making; and certainly cannot allocate corporate budgets. The buck stops at the desk of the SM and nowhere else.

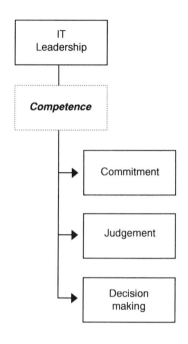

Figure 11.3 IT Leadership

Commitment

At the cultural level, it is important that the goals and objectives of the company are known, understood and supported by all the workforce, and that includes the top executives. When the IT project gets into trouble, and this is virtually certain to happen sooner or later, it is very pro-survival to know that there are some people in high places who are on your side and understand what you are doing. By and large, lack of SM competence implies lack of top-level commitment. And without top-level commitment – there can be no survival.

Judgement

In my office I have a reasonable number of books on IT development and on the strategic applications of IT. Yet, in none of the related indexes is there one mention of the term 'judgement'. This appears to be the case, even though good judgement is surely a critical faculty in assessing different strategic options and ways forward. The history of IT system development seems to be strewn with projects where one poor decision effectively kills off all subsequent work (it is all too often the first one that states: 'the company shall build an advanced and complex system...'). In order to exercise good judgement, there are at least two critical aspects that will be relevant: risk assessment and strategic alignment.

a) Risk assessment and control.

IT development has always been a high risk enterprise. It follows that anything that helps to limit or contain the problem has to be a significant strategic tool. However, risk management is still costly and labour intensive (and, dare one say it, *risky*) and there has to be clear support at all levels of the company for it to be effective. It will involve formal risk analysis at the corporate and project level followed by the preparation of fall-back proposals and recommendations to limit the exposure [13]. The skill then comes in choosing an agreed set of activities that will provide an *adequate* measure of security for a *reasonable* and cost-effective investment. It sounds straightforward but it is a far from easy task to trade off the uncertain benefits for a given cost.

b) Strategic alignment.

There is only one person who can truly assess IT system proposals and deliverables for conformance to the larger objectives of the organisation. That person is the chief executive. All it takes for good judgement is his or her profound understanding of the defined strategic goals, call them A, along with a clear vision of the proposed IT project deliverables, call them B. Then it needs a good analytical mind to establish whether B supports A or not. After that, the decision making is almost automatic.

Decision-making

Sitting on the fence here is roughly equivalent to corporate catalepsy. There may well be some desire to move, but nothing happens. In an ideal world, crises related to new or modified IT projects should get immediate visibility going up the chain of command, followed by a speedy set of viable work-rounds or solutions travelling down – all suitably agreed and signed off. This is the only way to get the project back on track. However if the managing director is not knowledgeable enough to directly handle the IT related problem, then he or she will have to seek assistance from, say, the heads of Marketing, Sales, Finance and perhaps even IT. They in turn will ask their minions for inputs, a few meetings will be held and the minutes eventually written up. Some sort of collective agreement will eventually rise to the top where a decision can then be made. This may be great consensus management but it is awful decision-making where strategic projects are concerned. A decision-maker who does not have a clear overview of the problem will rarely make good, effective, or timely decisions [14].

Structure

This section will provide an outline inventory of the factors that will potentially impact IT project planning and implementation. The object is to ensure that strategies can be optimised and decisions made while taking into account the existing format of the company. Without knowing that format, errors will surely follow. This section is more or less a laundry list of the organisation, which is not all that exciting. Nevertheless, such lists are of paramount value if, by chance, some laundry needs checking.

Corporate framework

It is not that there is a right or wrong way to run a company – there isn't, but it is important to find out what currently exists and correlate it with the current level of profitability. At one level, for example, if profit levels are good, then one can be sparing with new proposals for change. However, for most situations, it will be helpful to establish the status of the following corporate areas before committing the company to any new set of development activities:

❑ Does the company operate with centralised/decentralised management? In other words, to what extent is there local autonomy? [15];

❑ Is management hierarchical structure tall or wide? Are there many levels of management to the top, or only a few? [15];

❑ Is the IT network distributed or does it run on, say, a mainframe?

❑ Is the senior management competent in IT related matters?

❑ Is the IT director competent in IT matters? (N.B. any news, however bad, is still news);

❑ Has any inventory been undertaken of all the company IT hardware, operating systems, development tools, test facilities and application programs?

❑ What is the *true* success rate with IT system development over the years and across the organisation?

This is just a cross-section of one set of possible queries. The best approach for any organisation is to set up its own team which could then define and establish the right package of questions to be addressed by their own particular company.

Development environment

If the previous section defined the characteristics of the corporate structure, then this section will repeat the exercise for the IT development group. Some possible areas for inventory review could be:

❑ Existing processors and associated operating systems (e.g. Unix);

❑ Development tools and methodologies in current use (e.g. SSADM);

❑ In-house database systems (for example 'Oracle');

❑ Status of system test facilities;

❑ Current documentation strategy – or its absence.

And so on, and so on. Once again, it will be important to develop your own set of key questions to be addressed. The value here is that it will enable you to assess new IT development proposals in terms of current IT conditions and capabilities within the company.

System taxonomy

Again, this is not earth-shaking work, but it will be helpful to have a window looking across existing systems in current use and non-use in the organisation. The resultant groupings may help to point to successful current system applications, deadwood, or corporate exposures to be addressed with future work. There are six main groups active today:

❏ *Administration systems* The basic transaction type (e.g. Sales or Personnel data processing);

❏ *Executive system* The high-level information source (e.g. a Decision Support System based on the Sales data);

❏ *Network system* The approach that is configured for multi-users on a network to access the data (e.g. Europe-wide NT-4 users);

❏ *Data warehouses (and data-marts)* These are large (the marts) and extremely large databases. The huge scale calls for special methods to handle the data storage and retrieval problems [16];

❏ *Object Oriented system* These are systems where the OO design interacts with the relational model. They are not straightforward but they do handle graphic data (e.g. photos) very well [17];

❏ *Web-based system* This uses the web as the link (*hyperlink*) between the client user and the web server data-store [18].

The mechanics of these system structures are evolving rapidly, and some serious technical skill will be needed to understand the relative pros and cons of these system types. By and large, if you do not have the technical understanding, or strong support from, say, the IT director, then be wary of signing the budget approval slip.

Groupware

This is a set of modern communication techniques, internal to the organisation, that uses IT networks. In general terms, groupware is the software application(s) that enables people with some common interest, say, a project team, to communicate with each other. They will link up over a local or global computer network such that messages (verbal and written), proposals, plans, graphic images, reviews, and other documents can be sent to all other interested parties with the minimum of fuss, delay or cost. It is an exploding field of new information flow techniques and the SM will need to take an informed position of what is currently in use and what will need to be introduced. In turn, this may well shape future corporate strategy and investment [19]. The options include:

❏ *E-mail* Perhaps the most regularly used communication tool. Excellent message handler between two or more users, with the possibility to enclose 'attachments', i.e. text or graphic files;

❏ *Intranet* A non-interactive look-up facility which is only accessible to the workforce within the organisation. It is a 'for your eyes only' web site which can be used to establish the status of current research, or management changes, or strategic goals being implemented anywhere within the organisation;

❏ *Lotus 'Notes'* One of the first, very successful applications. It is a form of unstructured document database where the networked user can access and potentially modify the contents of each document;

❏ *Workflow* An application that will provide a planned flow of a document (file) from node to node. Thus, an electronic form could be moved round the company adding data at each stage: order_receipt; entry_date; credit_check; stock_status_of_items; unit_price_update; delivery_note; and so on;

❏ *Electronic document management* At the simplest level, this is the introduction of the 'paperless office' where every incoming document (graphic or text) is scanned, stored electronically, and the hard copy then sent to the archive or destroyed [20];

❏ *Conferencing* The use of telephonic and video techniques to enable a group meeting to take place electronically. Each work location will have a specially equipped room for this purpose and a meeting could involve participants from all five continents.

The investment per application, per user could be high – both in cost and culture shift impact, but, in terms of effective utilisation of a distributed workforce, it may be the only show in town.

Workforce skills

Before undertaking any new major activity, it will be worthwhile to examine and check-list the skills and level of expertise present in the organisation. Any gap or exposure could have a potential impact on future system planning.

To take a trite hypothetical example – assume that the development group proposes to implement your next IT system using a Windows NT 4 client/server platform (a Microsoft operating system). What operating system expertise do you need in-house in order to accept such a proposal? One possible minimalist corporate set of skills could be:

❏ *Senior management:* A top level awareness of the major pros and cons of NT-based applications;

❏ *IT management:* Knowledge of the necessary environment, standards, skills and practices that an NT platform development will call up;

❏ *Operations:* Competence in 'Visual Basic' and general experience of NT reliability, network traffic optimisation, debugging techniques, and possible malfunction work-rounds;

❏ *Test engineering:* Test specification experience and available operating test-equipment relevant to NT applications;

❏ *Quality department:* Capability of defining the documentation set and approval requirements related to an NT development regime;

❏ *Product management:* Ability to deliver realistic project estimates for an NT development exercise;

❏ *Maintenance:* Experience of handling NT failure modes, upgrading new software versions, tuning for performance, and adding or removing extra features.

Now assess the risk if, say, your test department only had experience in Unix software in a Mini configuration. Is this a serious or trivial problem? Can the department or the organisation handle it? How long would it take to get up to speed? Is it still a potential problem if the development centre offers to test it for you, anyway? How reliable would the test specifications then be? One thing is clear: if you ever sign a contract without resolving this or any other equivalent skill issue, you will be sitting on a volcano which is ready to blow at any instant.

Quality

Quality is generally considered the *sine qua non* of successful system development. However, in the context of this book, the conventional way of prioritising on the quality function is not going to help very much. We will see why this is so by broadly exploring three main avenues of quality application: software development (i.e. generating lines of working code);

the system development environment; and the impact on the overall organisation.

Quality application

For most purposes, a high quality rating implies the ability to deliver a product that will meet and continue to meet certain defined operational requirements. That is to say, it will work as promised and not break down – more than is absolutely necessary. For all that, the focus of interest will change for each specific application.

Lines of code   Here 'quality' is primarily related to 'defect rate' or the number of errors eliminated before hand-over of software to the user. Furthermore, if the 'quality' of a development program is poor, that program will suffer from unacceptable schedules or gross overspend [21].

System   For IT systems, there is one useful measure of the overall 'quality' of a development program: the maintenance cost after hand-over to the client. Naturally, some of that cost will be related to upgrades and additional system features (see 'maintenance' in Appendix 2) but the maintenance cost related to 'fixing' the system after delivery will establish the quality of the finished package. One source suggests that 30 billion dollars is spent per year on system maintenance alone and that it still comprises the major expense (i.e. more than 50% of project spend) for every system project [22].

Organisation   From the point of view of the organisation, 'quality' is an attitude of the workforce from the top level to the bottom. It is represented by a full commitment to address the needs of the customer, to sort out problems in a positive manner, and to minimise political infighting. And it has to be top down, where every layer of management in the organisation is seen to be actively supporting this culture [23].

Failure sources

Even in the above abridged form, all these variants of quality sound pretty powerful stuff, generating good code, low maintenance, and a solid human rapport. Yet, none of them is well suited to our purpose.

Consider again the four key problem areas uncovered in the development process for large systems:

❑ Initial requirements analysis in an IT development program can never be complete or accurate (Chapter 4);

❑ Planning the system development to meet long-term technical requirements will be virtually impossible due to the impact of 'change' and other inputs (Chapter 5);

❑ Initial estimates for schedules, costs and ROI (Return on Investment) are more or less worthless due to the above factors (Chapter 6);

❑ Non-technical top management personnel will have a significant impact on the development of IT systems, but do not always understand them (this chapter and Chapter 7).

Now let's return to the quality functions and see how they can help or reduce the importance of these failure modes. A first glance will show the obvious, that there is no sensible mapping between the quality programs outlined above and the problems related to the development process. To restate this, even if the all the quality targets discussed were *fully* met – perfect error-free code, etc. – there would still be absolutely no impact on the severe risks posed by the above four project problem areas.

Conclusion

So quality does not count, right? Wrong. There are clearly two possible routes to perdition and each one can take over from the other: either the project will suffer inherently as a long-term planning exercise, *or* the project will fail anyway due to poor quality objectives and procedures – say, starved test funding, or lack of documentation standards. So, undertaking successful system development has to be a two-stage affair:

❑ First solve the fundamental long-term problems discussed in this book. This will address inherent project failures, i.e. will the project ever survive the development phase (Chapter 7);

❑ Secondly, ensure that the new projects will be treated within an adequate quality environment. This will, hopefully, enable the system to continue working in an effective manner after delivery to the client.

Training

First, the easy one: why is staff training to be considered a strategic item? Because, in its absence, the shortage of modern skills will rapidly degrade the competitive capabilities of the organisation [24]. For all that, even if the need is clear, the problem of who pays for this strategic service is still something of an open question. The employer, here, is in a no-win situation. After training, an employee will have increased his or her value in the job market and may well take the new training and run. Conversely, if no training is considered, the workforce, along with the organisation, will become an obsolete commodity within the space of a few years [25]. To lay down effective staff enhancement programs and implement actual training courses may call for some careful thinking. Nevertheless, regardless of risk – in the long run something will have to be done.

In principle, there are two potential sources to be evaluated, in-house and external, and either of these can be called on to deliver different types of training: technical, managerial, and executive. They are all important, but this section will concentrate on the last one.

The executive model

Before any training program can be set up, you have to decide what the final objective is to be. On that basis, consider the following possible proposal for the executive environment at the opening of the new millennium:

> Assumption: that the future of IT development will continue to be fast paced, rapidly changing due to new market and technology breakthroughs, along with increased competitive stress at a global level. Powerful new communication and marketing channels, challenging product performance requirements, new complex development tools, pressure to minimise costs and increasing demands to reduce time-scales: all these will be the norm for the system development environment.

If this prognosis sounds at all realistic, then clearly there will be little place for the classical structured approach in commercial IT development management. 'Long-term strategic-planning' will become another example of an oxymoron and all the book's pointers to the death (or near-terminal condition) of the long-term project will have been realised. This was first discussed in Chapter 9. Can there be any future for the structured methodology? Outside of local and central government agencies, I do not see it, but there is always scope for further argument. So where does all this leave the executive – what strategic tools and mechanisms does he need in order to operate successfully in this swirling, fast-changing, ever-new, uncertain environment? This is covered in more detail in Chapter 12, but we can pre-empt some of the discussion here:

> The essential executive capabilities will need to be short-term, flexible and opportunistic. The senior management will always have to be ready – now run, now stop, now reverse in any given direction – depending purely on market, technical and corporate conditions at any one time. The processes, procedures and tools needed for fast development will be in place and available for immediate application, or replacement. Management will be based on a 'game' plan rather than formal planning [26].

This represents the basic required 'senior manager' model for the near future which can now be used to establish the training requirements.

Executive training

There have been 3 strands of IT management training needs so far :

❑ The question of competence covered in Figure 11.3;

❑ The fourth key problem defined 2 pages back; and

❑ The required future needs discussed on the previous page.

Overall, it is taken as a strategic imperative that the senior management must be capable of reviewing, at some suitable level, all IT options for fast decision making, for problem resolution and for forward corporate planning.

Training objective

Training will enable non-IT executives to become familiar with most of the following list (add or remove items as required):

❑ The main strategies of modern IT system development;

❑ Pros and cons of current development methodologies;

❑ The impact of modifications to formal requirement documents;

❑ Scope and limitation of software test regimes;

❏ Graphic tools used to model IT systems;

❏ The output data provided by the Project Management team;

❏ Current status of computer and communications equipment;

❏ The technical skills available in-house;

❏ Existing hardware and software development tools.

Training implementation

If the above or similar work format is accepted, then the details of the actual training regime can be agreed between the parties. But the minimum set of requirements will usually need:

❏ the enthusiastic support of the trainee(s);

❏ the study format, to be set up on a weekly basis, say, 1 to 4 hours;

❏ the delivery to be defined: video, computer-based, or face-to-face;

❏ the special needs of the specific executive(s); and

❏ the duration, expected to be between 6 and 18 months to complete.

Summary

This section has concentrated only on the executive part of the training program. However, it is only one part of the overall package, and it is important to recognise that the difference between good training planning and implementation and bad or no training will be considerable. The long-term viability of the organisation will always depend on two items: a) the quality and competence of the staff; and b) the focused training that will translate this competence into meeting specific strategic goals.

Stress

This is a fairly modern issue. Twenty years ago, there was virtually no consideration given to stress as a factor of staff employment. However, today, it would be more than prudent to ensure that current levels of stress in the organisation are: a) monitored; and b) kept to within acceptable limits. In this light, a recent news item reported an epidemic of city workers visiting their dentist. Apparently, they were continually grinding their teeth due to their stressful jobs and fear of redundancy [27]. Unless it is lightly applied, which is rare, the general impact of stress will be strongly and consistently counter-productive. It will frequently lead to increased absenteeism, a substantial rise in smoking, drinking and/or drug abuse, reduced morale, added error injection in the work deliverables (deliberate or accidental), reduced production output, and a degraded social environment in the workplace and at home. Modern-day stresses seem to come in all shapes and sizes and will usually apply to all levels of management – up to and including the chief executive. They will include :

Corporate structure

Every time another layer of management is removed, the level and range of responsibilities for the existing managers has to be increased to cover for the staff that had left. At some point the manager goes into overload with a dramatic loss of productivity [28].

Technology

Today's rate of change in work-practice is dramatically high. The staff need to be adept at handling the latest computer hardware (suitably networked), administration systems, various application software and associated handbooks (each package modified every 18 months), the printer and its consumables, fax, e-mail, groupware, and web sites. Most people in the office more or less know about some of the equipment by the time it is replaced, but the never-ending upgrades and related training packages can seriously reduce the self-confidence and morale of most of the office staff.

Job security

The fear of loss of work is not particularly new, but it is more evident today for two main reasons:

Objectives   The company today sees a loss of personnel, usually via computer system applications, as a positive competitive goal. Business process re-engineering, downsizing, rightsizing, and merging all have the same objective, and it is not one guaranteed to reduce individual stress;

Age   In the UK there is an employment culture that technical managers and their cohorts should be young in both appearance and outlook. Which is fine. But today's successful thirty-somethings may soon be tomorrow's forty-unemployables. And that thought in itself can be stressful.

The above two factors have led to a culture of taking on an ever-increasing workload; working at home; and coming in at the weekends. All this in the hope that your colleague will be selected for the next 'Dear John' from the HR department, and you will be reprieved until the next time [29].

Work visibility

Currently, there is an interesting re-enactment of the time-and-motion studies of the late nineteenth century. It is called the 'Call Centre' and it is, without question, a profitable exercise. It has become a useful source of employment and, further, it addresses one of today's key commercial requirements – effective liaison with the customer. So what is the problem? The problem is that the computerised technology involved enables the work of a call centre operative to be monitored minutely throughout the day. As a result, there is a considerable burnout factor and staff turnover levels are correspondingly high [30]. This represents, perhaps in an exaggerated form, the situation to be found increasingly in most commercial offices today.

Messaging

An interesting study released by Pitney Bowes [31] explores the way in which various modern methods of office communications have impacted the work habits of the manager. The switch to remote colleague locations (other sites, teleworkers) or absence from the desk (meetings, travel) requires an increase in impersonal messages using e-mail, voice-mail, and the fax. The study suggests that the average office worker sends or receives more than a 100 messages a day and these messages constitute a significant, unwanted and very stressful addition to the daily workload. People, it would seem, prefer speech or direct contact with the person sharing the communication.

Bullying

The relatively conventional form of bullying relates to a high-positioned sad case (SC) making the life of one or more of this individual's staff miserable. It could be related to a poor childhood, total personal inadequacy or a pathological dislike of, say, foreigners, women, or elderly personnel. In any case, it is unpleasant and should be eradicated. An alternative approach of the SC is to send an abusive e-mail (flame-mail) to the selected victim(s) which generally manages to move the recipient's productivity to yet another notch lower [32]. Another relatively new and totally unwelcome addition to the workplace is someone called the 'overloaded bully', currently being investigated by Professor Cooper of the Manchester School of Management [33]. This bully is largely the product of an unacceptably harsh work regime who responds to overload by pressuring the people beneath him or her. The result is a spreading pool of grief and frustration down to all levels of management. Like all the other forms, not recommended.

In summary, stress is not yet a critical issue for most companies. But it would be a foolhardy CEO who chose to ignore the potential impact of stress on his organisation.

Summary

The emphasis here has been to analyse the entire organisation for the personal attention of the senior management. Only then can long ranging decisions be made with fast turnaround and with a good probability of achieving a successful outcome. In short, the following points should be addressed:

❑ The non-technical Senior Management (SM) are ultimately responsible for all IT system projects undertaken. Theirs is the foremost strategic role in the entire exercise;

❑ The structure and inter-working of the workforce may have an important bearing on the collective output and should be carefully monitored for any apparent mis-match between parties;

❑ The SM must be capable of understanding IT techniques, approaches and issues and linking them to the overall strategic goals. Without this understanding, related decision-making may be critically delayed;

❑ In order to optimally apply the resources of the organisation, an inventory should be organised of all the strengths and gaps in the expertise of the IT workforce, their hardware equipment and the in-house software applications;

❏ Quality will have only a negligible impact in resolving the primary issues of long-term system development. However, once those issues have been resolved, the full application of quality techniques and processes will have a major bearing on the subsequent success of the project;

❏ In a fast moving market environment, ongoing IT training is a key weapon in maintaining the organisation's competitive position. It is applicable at all levels, but will be most crucial for senior management;

❏ Over the last few years, stress in line managers has become an important strategic factor. Stress acts to severely curtail the morale, involvement and pride of the workforce in achieving corporate objectives. The monitoring and containment of such stresses, therefore, will be of considerable value in maintaining an acceptable and enjoyable work environment for the staff.

References

1 Machiavelli N, The Prince, *(see under Bibliography)*

2 Hammer M, The Re-Engineering Revolution, Harper Collins, 1995

3 Bradbury D, A process of elimination, Computer Weekly, 31.7.1997, p. 33

4 Earl M, Management Strategies for Information Technology, p.2, Prentice Hall, 1989

5 Toffler A, Future Shock, Chapter 16, Pan Books, 1971

6 Hatley R, Telework could save a billion, The Times, "Interface" section, p.9. 16.7.1997

7 Robson W, Strategic Management and Information Systems, 2nd ed., p.457, Pitman, 1997

8 Collins T, Report reveals what users really think about outsourcing, Computer Weekly, 9.11.1995, p.16

9 Gracie S, Problem? Call in the troubleshooters, The Sunday Times, Business section, 21.2.1999, p.13

10 McConnell S, Rapid Development, Case Study 3.1, p.29, *(see under Bibliography)*

11 Yourdon E, Death March, p.2, *(see under Bibliography)*

12 Bosses Fear IT, says staff, Computing, 12.9.1996, p.33

13 McConnell S, Rapid Development, Chapter 5, *(see under Bibliography)*

14 Cooke S and Slack N, Making Management Decisions, p.4, Prentice Hall, 1991

15 Baron R, Behaviour in Organisations, p.432, Allyn and Bacon, 1986

16 Connolly T and Begg C, Database Systems 2nd Ed., Chapter 25, Addison-Wesley, 1999

17 Satzinger J and Orvik T, The Object Oriented Approach, p.134, *(see under Bibliography)*

18 Connolly T and Begg C, Database Systems 2nd Ed., Chapter 24, Addison-Wesley, 1999

19 Orfali R, Harkey D and and Edwards J, The Essential Client/Server Survival Guide 2ⁿᵈ Ed, Chapters 20,21, Wiley, 1996

20 Business guide to Electronic Document Management, Information Age, January 1999, p.25

21 McConnell S, Rapid Development, p.69, *(see under Bibliography)*

22 Parikh G, Techniques of Program and System Maintenance, p.29, QED Information Science, 1988

23 Massey J, Cultural resolutions, Computing, 23.2.1995, p.30

24 Barber J, Skills vacuum due to training decline, Computing, 11.5.1995, p.42

25 Hatzakis H, Viewpoint, Computing, 15.7.1999, p.24

26 Stacey R, Dynamic Strategic Management for the 1990s, Chapter 1, *(see under Bibliography)*

27 Metro (London), Stressed workers grind their teeth, 21.6.1999, p5

28 System breakdown, Computer Weekly, 5.2.1998, p.34

29 McGinn J, Under pressure, Computing, 16.10.1997, p.62

30 Mortished C, The Times (London), 17.4.1998, p.29

31 Pitney Bowes study finds messaging creates greater stress at work www.pitneybowes.com/pbi/whatsnew/releases/messaging_1998.htm

32 Kay J, The devil you know, Computer Weekly, 19.3.1998, p.46

33 Edwards M, £1.3 billion cost of new-style office tyrants, Evening Standard (London), 22.7.1999, p.9

Chapter 12   Wrap-up

Introduction

It has been a long journey, but this is where we can pull all the logical threads together that have been spun out in the preceding pages. The following two sections of the chapter will take a look back through the book to highlight the main points that have been covered in the past 200 odd pages. The fourth section will address one of the more serious questions still unanswered by the system development industry – the question of system utility. And, as a grand finale, we shall then explore some of the more intriguing strategic possibilities that could be applied in some future evolution of system development.

State of play

For the very last time, as a reminder, we can summarise the key points that will apply to virtually all new IT system development projects.

Current status

It is worth stressing yet again that, for IT system development, all the conventional management strategies, methodologies, and development tools now in use in the new millennium are roughly as inadequate as they were for the mid 1960s mainframe applications. Only the cost has risen. The probability of these current systems meeting their original objectives continues to be very much lower than 50%. In order to bring some measure of commercial benefit (or fiscal probity) into these products, something, somewhere will have to get a lot better.

Feasibility study

Almost by definition, a feasibility study for a new IT system project will be carried out by a limited workforce in a limited timeframe and cover new or significantly upgraded hardware and software. Again, almost by definition, there is virtually no possibility that the key aspects of this new project can be securely captured by such a team. For most projects, it will not even be possible to identify the impending key problem areas until much later in the program.

Planning

Long range planning in a highly volatile environment hardly ever produces cost-effective results. Anything that nullifies the original planning assumptions must also nullify any outputs or objectives that result from such planning. This automatically calls for rework. This problem will apply to nearly all projects under the control of, among others, central government, local government, and the armed services. Since the bulk of these organisations have to run large long-term projects, the delivered results should not be too surprising [1].

Forecasting

Forecasting has three principal functions: a) to identify all the activities and sub-elements that will be needed to develop a product; b) to estimate all the elapsed times that these activities will take; and c) to establish the cost of delivering the final assembled product to the client. In a long range project, the accuracy of such estimated values must fall close to zero. This is because changing conditions, outside either control or meaningful assessment, will continue to drastically modify all the above three parameters.

Project environment

There is a check list (summarised in Table 3.1 at the end of Chapter 3) of some of the basic 'rules' or patterns that can lead a project to potential failure. All the previous paragraphs will apply if a project is a long term exercise (Rule 5). However, even if the project is suitably short term, say, 9 months, if it starts out with any of the other five rules being applicable, then the project is still probably in a great deal of trouble (for example, Rule 6: 'if the objectives are poorly defined then the project will fail').

Leadership

The 3 most important factors to be addressed in any system development project are: the inherent long-range failure modes; the poor project environment (for example, lack of quality); and finally, the non-technical senior management. Perhaps they, the management, are *the* most important factor as they have the power to define both the operational range and the environment of a project. In any case, such management needs a good understanding of the strategic value of IT systems and the problems that will be met in system development. Only then will they be able to take a leadership role in IT planning and budget allocation. In addition, it will allow timely and effective decisions to be made in resolving the day-to-day problems of such development exercises.

The strategic upgrade

In order to break part of the log-jam produced by the above development operating conditions, some high-level changes to the organisation's culture, management structure and operating procedures may need to be carried out. Once the problems have been clearly understood, it is just a matter of finding and then applying the right solutions tailored to suit the needs of the individual organisations.

Design philosophy

One of the most obvious messages from Part 2 was that long-term projects carry with them the seeds of their own failure. Solution: stop planning or developing long-term projects. This is easier to state than to actually carry out. In general, such a move calls for a carefully planned three part approach: first, obtain broad agreement on the corporate need to make such changes; secondly evaluate the many RAD options (see Appendix 2) and decide on one; and, finally, institute a whole package of dedicated training courses that will prepare the company's workforce for using the new approach in, maybe, 18 months to 2 years time. (Any less time and there will be gaps in the staff's competence – they will know the material, but not at a professional level.)

In parallel with the new fast-track development method, prepare to take on pilot testing, modular structures and incremental design objectives (see Chapter 9). Again, these will need to be carefully integrated as all of them will test the flexibility of the company as it undergoes various shifts in outlook and culture.

Organisational structure

One of the major problems in system development lies in the need for good communication networks (the human variety). A project may have effectively died two years ago, but the company could still be pumping funds into it because no-one has monitored or understood or reported the project manager's output. This communication breakdown can be tackled by generating multiple information paths up and down the chain of command, by holding regular (and irregular) status audits, by implementing a change control board, by laying down proper levels of corporate documentation, and by setting up a climate where bad news can be safely delivered. Under these circumstances, there is a far better chance that the required data will get through and any necessary corrective action can then be undertaken.

Management

The non-IT senior management have a crucial role to play in the development process. They, and no-one else, control all aspects of corporate strategy, decision-making and funding. It is, therefore, critically important that the SM possess an understanding of IT systems, their potential impact, and the development processes involved in creating them. In addition, in an ideal world, there should be a good rapport between the SM and the IT manager, director or CIO. It goes without saying, they should also be competent and motivated general managers.

There are three main criteria to be satisfied if the SM are to make effective and timely contributions with regard to IT developments. The first is that they should be committed, i.e. support the main thrust of applying IT systems as an important strategic tool. The second is that they should be knowledgeable about IT related concepts and current levels of IT product capabilities. Finally, they should be aware of the overall state of IT standards, development practices and applications as presently carried out within the organisation. In all likelihood, dedicated training courses will need to be planned and undertaken to reach this level of competence.

Strategic upgrade summary

There has never been a way to guarantee success in the field of IT system development. With the continued investment of serious money and good minds over the years, the global failure rates are still unacceptably high. However, a number of possible strategic solutions do exist and these could potentially benefit any organisation which possesses the determination to apply them at all levels.

The test-case study

As a final act of looking back, this is a good time to re-examine the case study first given in Chapter 1 on page 7. There it was suggested that you put down a few proposals on how to handle the project 'Trawlerman'. As a reminder, the key facts are repeated below:

> This development project was approved by the UK Ministry of Defence in 1988. It was to provide an administrative system capable of handling classified information. The date for operational delivery was to be 1991, but, in the event, hand-over did not occur until 1993 and the system was not fully operational until 1995. At which point, the system was declared obsolete and the decision was made to scrap the entire application. The cost of the development was in the region of £40 million.

The question posed in Chapter 1 was: if you were in overall charge of UK military expenditure at that time, i.e. 1995, what steps, if any, would you now recommend? If you did write down some ideas at that time, then (before looking at the proposals lower down) try again now to see if your view or approach to solving this project problems has altered.

One possible format for an answer could be:

❑ Assumption: that there was still a need for the product;

❏ Analysis: the senior manager involved was most likely an 'amateur' (Chapter 7) since the project was stopped only after all the expensive work had been finished;

❏ Prognosis: rework (2nd time round – see 'winning failures' in Chapter 8) would most likely succeed as all the feasibility studies, system analysis, coding and documentation were now fully signed off and available for upgrading for possible upgrading and simplification;

❏ Possible summary proposals for a rework cycle:

- Put someone in charge with proven IT competence;

- Modify to a low-cost commercial application;

- Request a full project proposal within 4 weeks;

- If OK, provide a further £8 million and 6 months to complete.

Note that such an approach does not guarantee success. Further, there could be other better proposals. However, at least with this set of proposals, the down-side is limited. In the first instance, a low cost 4 week review period is given. Only if the resulting report is accepted will a further extension be permitted. Having already spent £40 million, the added total exposure is for another 20% of the initial cost. Again, the time scale is such that external change factors are unlikely to interfere with the main objectives. And the project team will be very familiar with the current project goals, documents and problem areas. Perhaps the most important proposal is the first since a good experienced manager will bring some much-needed expertise to the project. On balance, it has a good chance to succeed if all the above recommendations were followed and the documentation from the previous development exercise is available.

System utility

This book would not be complete without a serious overview of the corporate value of IT systems. Or the absence of value. So let's travel lightly here, with a more reflective, philosophical approach. And for the moment, let's ignore the possibility of failure – against all the odds, let's assume that a planned system project has been developed, installed and effectively applied by the grateful end-users.

Up to now, even successful IT system development is seen to create awkward cultural shifts, technical upheavals, significant cost increases, maintenance overload and general stress throughout the organisation. Nevertheless, in spite of all these problems, it is usually assumed that it is an enterprise well worth undertaking. Such work is expected to provide some quantifiable form of bottom-line profit or measurable competitive advantage. This section will now test that expectation and analyse the evidence to see if the hypothesis generally holds true.

To attack the problem, there are four major areas to be investigated: development costs, performance metrics, system value and corporate benefit, and it may help to provide them with a few simple definitions:

❑ *Costs* The total outlay undertaken before and after installation of the new system. This will include the added hardware and software, office facilities, extra personnel, development, test, installation, training and system maintenance. In a phrase: the Total Cost of Ownership or TCO;

❑ *Performance* Some definition of test format that will enable the system capabilities to be measured against some standard criteria;

❑ *Value* An agreed set of monitors for business performance will have to be set up. Ideally, subsequent results with the new system should then be compared with the original commercial capabilities before the new system. The object is to obtain the 'return on investment' or ROI;

❑ *Benefit* Another model, this time to assess the degree by which the system application has moved the strategic objectives forward. In other words, providing 'competitive advantage'.

Development costs

There is no way that the 'value' or the 'benefit' of a system can be evaluated without a clear knowledge of the cost of development and application. To underline this, take a simple hypothetical example:

> Assume that a treatment were available that would truly guarantee that the patient would never suffer from any form of cancer. Now further assume that the cost of this treatment was, say, £500 (or dollars, or euros). Most, but not all, people would pay up happily. As an insurance policy, it is well within range of most people's pockets. Now assume that the asking price was amended to £500,000. Same

product, same guarantee, but this time – most, but not all, people would not pay up. The cost would be simply too high.

It may be obvious, but there is little harm in emphasising that cost is an important strategic parameter. This topic was last aired in Chapter 6 – and things have not changed much since. The discussion then was with regard to the 'business plan' and now we are concerned with the overall costs of the project. But in the end, the conclusion is going to be pretty much the same – unless your company owns a rare and meticulous costing department with appropriate reporting procedures in place across every resource in the company, you will not get very far in capturing the project costs. Perhaps the first control point in managing expenditure is the overall IT budget and the priority project allocations. A recent survey carried out with IT directors and managers suggested that they had only limited knowledge or interest in the annual budget. In the large company group (500 or more employees) nearly one fifth of those asked did not know if their total budget allocation had changed from the previous year [2]. There is not even a consensus on the right philosophy for handling IT related costs: the TCO or 'Total Cost of Ownership' is now an obsolete technique [3], while the TCO offers a valid way forward in monitoring overall expenses [4]. You choose.

Performance metrics

This is another of these key factors that is hard to quantify but will still cause the end-users to down tools if unsatisfactory (see Chapter 3). The performance criteria could relate to some measure of the IT system itself, or, better still, to the business sector which is served by the application.

Measuring performance

Establishing the meaningful performance of an IT system in isolation is not all that easy. It is relatively simple to provide a test vehicle for modelling the product, but the problem lies in the relationship between the measurement model and the real world application. Any system can have large variations in: data traffic levels between the system and the users, the tuning range of the database required to meet varying inputs, different types of database query structures, skills (and training and aptitude) of the end-user, and upgrades of the operating system and database software. All these, among many others, may cause a significant change in overall performance. In the case of monitoring the business usage it is, of course, much worse. The whole impact of the IT system could be masked or accentuated by other elements of the business process, by different strategic inputs such as a marketing campaign, or by external changes, e.g. an economic downturn.

Balanced scorecard

One way out of this whole mess is to spread the performance measurements across a whole range of selected business parameters. The 'balanced scorecard' sets out to do just this and was put forward by Kaplan and Norton [5]. In it, they proposed to measure performance based on four (five) major areas of the business: finance; customer; innovation; internal processes; (and employees). Each of these areas is further broken down into key sectors for measurement and the overall result is obtained from compounding the outputs of all these measures [5, 6]. This balanced card technique is well supported by some large companies in general industry, but, as usual, it is not all sweetness and light – and there is definitely no silver bullet [7, 8]. Before jumping, make sure that the following factors have been assessed and covered:

❑ Clear need in organisation;

❑ High cost of corporate introduction (learning curve);

❑ Evaluation and in-house accord on the suitable measurement set;

❑ Framework definition, e.g. is IT part of the scorecard?

❑ Continuous review and upgrade contents of scorecard;

❑ Other techniques required for big changes (Japan's trade in 90s);

❑ Current scorecard nullified with new partnerships and alliances;

❑ Scorecard has poor utility in dynamic trading conditions.

Application response measurement (ARM)

This is something slightly different: an approach for actually measuring the system response at the transactional level while in operational use. ARM has, at one and the same time, some powerful advantages in terms of generating solid performance confidence, along with some equally depressing disadvantages in setting it up [9]. Once again it is over to you.

Advantages   There is a standard supported by the Computer Measurement Group and some large users.

It generates an accurate measure of transactional performance in the user environment.

Provides a proof that the performance will meet the Service Level Agreement (SLA) requirements.

Disadvantages It involves writing new added (debugged and tested and documented) code to monitor the transaction.

The application vendors have shown little enthusiasm for adding this extra code.

It is still early days, and so far there has been little demand by the users for such capabilities.

System value

What is the value of creating an intranet for the organisation? Should you have spent good money on a Y2K project? How long is a piece of string? Answering the third question is not too bad: measure it to the required level of accuracy. The second question is the easiest: at the time, there was no choice – just get on with it for the lowest possible expenditure. But the first is a bit of a problem. In the first instance, as discussed above, there is no clear guideline to the anticipated costs for creating such a product. And even if you know the cost, the return on investment (ROI) – now that is really difficult to measure operationally. How can you quantify the return on this new intranet product which is probably being introduced into the organisation at the same time as some other systems, a new declared strategy on groupware, a 5% downsizing in personnel, and a shift in the external market? The truth is, there is rarely any clear answer or means to arrive at an answer. In two major surveys – carried out by different organisations and separated by more than 9 years – more than 65% of the top corporate managers addressed admitted that they had no way to measure the ROI on IT related activity [10, 11].

You can jump, you can use your experience, you can trust to the judgement of others, you can invest in analytical packages or decision support software, you can limit exposure to a certain percentage of the company's turnover, but in the end an IT investment is always going to be something of a gamble. There is no formulaic approach to establishing the value of corporate IT projects.

Corporate benefit

As a prelude to the next section, we can look at some of the surveys spread over the last decade that have addressed the question of organisational benefit.

❏ A research study in 1990 from the Imperial College, London, suggests that most users will not obtain any tangible (or intangible) benefit from their IT system investment. The 'competitive advantage' so frequently sought after is something of a mirage and very few managers will have the skill, luck or foresight to actually achieve it [12].

❏ The impact of computers on productivity has been studied by Professor Tom Landauer of the University of Colorado. He arrives at the pessimistic view that, in spite of appearances, computers are not user-friendly (and therefore are not used effectively) and do not provide adequate features (and therefore do not improve user productivity) [13].

❏ A survey from the PA Consulting group suggests that most organisations do not get any real benefit from investing in workgroup processes. This is in spite of optimistic claims of considerable improvements in productivity using such products [14].

❏ A book by Carrington and Llanguth, *The Banking Revolution: Salvation or Slaughter* (Financial Times Management, 1997), looks at 15 years of investment wastage by the UK banking sector. The authors suggest that there is little in terms of productivity to show for the billions (literally) spent on IT banking systems [15].

The Strassmann factor

There are not many workers in IT strategy who deserve a named heading, but I guess Paul Strassmann could be one of them.

Figure 12.1 is based on his work and is a representation of a graphic plot linking the IT investment of companies (as a percentage of revenue) to the return on corporate assets. The dotted line is what you would tend to expect: a higher investment in IT ('spend') should give a corresponding improved competitive advantage in the market place leading in turn to a higher return on assets.

But this is not what Strassmann found. Each of a few hundred companies was studied for its particular return on assets for a given IT investment and the result would then be plotted as a dot on the graph. The bulk of these dots were found to fit more or less randomly into the grey rectangle – indicating that the return on assets was reasonably constant and independent of the level of investment. The interesting thing is that the shape of the grey plot is sensibly the same for two entirely different sets of data plotted from hundreds of company results. The first was obtained in the middle 80s and the later one in the middle 90s [16, 17].

This is not a black or white issue. There are questions about the actual measures of profitability, but this is fully discussed in one of his books: *The Squandered Computer* (Information Economics Press, 1997). There are also a number of voices in disagreement (see the discussion in [16]) but, at the very least, perhaps Figure 12.1 should be kept in mind when fixing the next budget allocation.

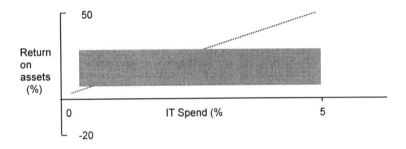

Figure 12.1   IT spend and return on assets (after Strassmann)

Overview

These last few pages have tried to capture the utility of IT based systems at the level of the organisation. It is still difficult to define the related parameters, to isolate the effect of every modification to the corporate model, or to establish a clear correlation between computer usage and bottom-line profitability. All this, and recall that the initial assumption was the successful outcome of the system development work – which is still far from the truth in the majority of cases.

Life goes on. Companies will rightly continue to plan and develop new network structures, new web applications, new datamarts, new security frameworks, and new integrated enterprise systems. For all that, it is hoped that the last few pages will give some pause for reflection.

Future strategy

This section will try to take on board all the findings outlined to date, i.e. the proposals discussed in Part 3 of the book. It will be divided into 2 parts: a framework for development work that reflects modern changing conditions; and a set of possible corporate modifications that would enable such work to be carried out effectively.

Framework

❏ Today's model of the organisation, the market place, or the product development cycle is not deterministic (more poke, more yelp) but non-linear and complex (more poke, maybe yelp, maybe purr, maybe something else). This is a chaos-like property where a small incremental shift in input operating conditions could make a huge disproportionate change in output result due to the finer and finer granularity of the change map. (Moving the location of the input position – the star – from left to right across the rectangle will change its background from white to black , and back again – see Figure 12.2.)

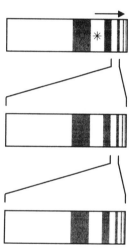

Figure 12.2
The change map

❏ The traditional approach to development modelling assumes that the working environment is essentially stable and it will be enough to define all the major steps and related activities at the outset. Changes during development are assumed to be non-existent or minimal. At the worst, they will only happen occasionally (top part of Figure 12.3).

❏ The improvisational model assumes that the strategic environment is dynamic and continuously changing. All planning, therefore, has to be short term and *ad-hoc*, with a rapid-response capability (the bottom part of Figure 12.3).

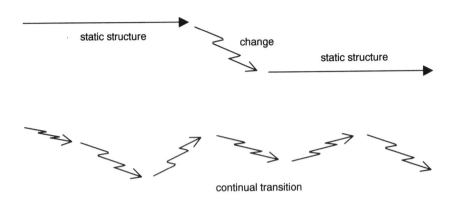

Figure 12.3   Approaches to system environment

❑ Companies that have introduced a flexible, adaptable culture with good change-management techniques will have a significant competitive advantage in a fast-moving market place.

❑ Development will continue to be high-risk and adrenalin-pumping. Close controls should be introduced to reduce the downside potential to an acceptable level. Discovery-driven planning is one approach that tackles this issue [21]. It assumes that the bulk of the planning data will only become available as the project progresses. Therefore repeated audits to check status and, if necessary, to cancel the project are used to minimise risk in an uncertain environment. In addition, it looks for the hidden assumptions that underpin the investment in a particular project. These assumptions are then carefully analysed for ongoing validity.

❑ Good top-level management will be needed in a changing environment to limit the stress on the workforce to acceptable levels.

Recommendations

This is a huge subject and we have only touched the surface. Risks are high, investments are higher, and perhaps you have no choice. For more information you can refer to [18-23] and you could also consider the following strategies for possible application:

❏ *Hit Team* Set up a highly trained hit team, an SAS type group (Strategic Application Strikeforce?) as a crisis resource. This could be thrown in to examine and report on the strategic impact of any new technology or pending market transition;

❏ *Culture* Plan to introduce a change-relevant culture to the organisation. This would encourage RAD rather than SSADM; perhaps OO development rather than relational structures; flexible managerial relationships rather than fixed responsibilities; and a supportive senior management approach to the workforce;

❏ *Training* Implement a full-scale training strategy where all management will be expected to acquire, maintain and upgrade their skills in new required technologies and methodologies;

❏ *Decisions* Provide an environment where fast decisions and faster budget amendments are expected as a strategic necessity;

❏ *Communications* Ensure that feedback from external suppliers, customers and competitors is marshalled to the right locations in the organisation. Further, ensure that in-house information flows do not suffer from traffic bottlenecks as they are channelled from department to department;

❏ *Alliances* Participate in shared developments with competitors (the alliance could be temporary or product related). This can prove a powerful instrument in the reduction of risk when introducing or marketing a new product;

❏ *Autonomic groups* Where new innovative products are being considered, prepare to set up largely-independent entrepreneurial groups loosely attached to the mother company. Only then can they compete effectively with other low-cost start-up organisations [23].

The unfolding challenge

In effect, for the reader, this point is now the beginning. To recap for the moment, the book's title suggests that there is a need to strengthen and support the development process associated with IT systems. This has been largely borne out by the formal analyses given in the earlier part of the book. In Part 1, the general discussion showed that most reported long-term development programs have been costly exercises with little benefit or pay-back to show for all the activity undertaken. In Part 2, the underlying causes of four decades of low project success rates were investigated. The results were shown to be mainly due to the impact of change-mechanisms on the project framework. In Part 3, some proposed solutions, work-rounds and damage-limitation exercises were explored for possible application.

Nevertheless, it is not all over – a number of useful questions have been posed, and some answers obtained. But, even now in the third millennium, problem areas are still very much present:

❏ The non-technical Senior Management are ultimately responsible for the success, or otherwise, of any IT system development. Without their constructive attitude, open commitment and regularly upgraded training, decisions will not be optimised, projects will remain at risk and success rates are likely to remain low (Chapters 7 and 11).

❏ Questions related to the cost, value, benefit and comparative analysis of strategic undertakings are still not satisfactorily resolved. Effective monitoring tools do not seem to be in place and estimates tend to be arbitrary and unreliable (Chapters 6 and 12).

❏ In order to raise development success rates, the culture, objectives and management structure of the organisation will probably have to be seriously modified (Chapter 10 and 11). These are major exercises, they will need a lot of planning and will cost heavily in stress, resource and time (for one possible approach, see the discussion in Appendix 1).

❏ Current methodologies are based on project planning being carried out in a largely steady-state environment. There is an increasing body of evidence which suggests that a fast-changing dynamic environment is more reflective of the current market. If this is true, it will require a radical change from a static to a more opportunistic strategic outlook. In turn, this may call for a well trained fast-response workforce and management capability (Chapter 12).

In other words, this book has highlighted some of the realities of today and indicated the major problem areas that remain to be addressed – along with some possible comments and hints on how to tackle them. There is still much work to be done.

As stated above, for the reader – this point is now the beginning.

References

1 UK's NAO report highlights defence projects delays, costs overruns, www.defence-data.com/current/page4699.htm
2 Lewis M, Fuddled by the figures, Computer Weekly, 5.8.1999, p.20
3 Riley J, Proving IT's worth, Computer Weekly, 25.2.1999, p.18
4 Harrington T, Total cost of ownership – the search goes on to locate IT's holy grail, Computing, 24.6.1999, p.26
5 Kaplan R and Norton D, The Balanced Scorecard: Translating Strategy into Action, Harvard Business School Press, 1996
6 Balanced Business Scorecard, metabpr.com/bbs.htm
7 Pringle D, Measure for Measure, Information Strategy, September 1998, p.28
8 Meredith S, Measuring IT's vital statistics, Computing, 27.5.1999, p.32
9 Goodwin C, Taking the measure of ARM's method, Computing, 29.7.1999, p.22
10 Harvey D, What's in it for the business?, Computer Weekly, 5.10.1989, p.22
11 Can IT count on the bottom line?, Computer Weekly, 10.12.1998, p.57
12 Researchers blow myth of competitive advantage, Computing, 1.11.1990, p.4
13 Landauer T, The Trouble with Computers: Usefulness, Usability, and Productivity, MIT Press, 1966
14 Bicknell D, Computers 'hinder productivity', Computer Weekly, 29.6.1995, p.2
15 Sabbagh D, Bankers count the cost, Computing, 16.10.97, p.1
16 Strassmann P, Will big spending on computers guarantee profitability?, Datamation, www.datamation.com/PlugIn/issues/1997/feb/02align.html
17 McAteer J, Measuring the return on Information Technology, p.2, SRI International Business Intelligence Program D95-1964, Nov. 1995
18 Orlikowski W, and Hofman J, An Improvisational Model of Change Management, Sloan Management Review, Winter 1997
19 Pringle G, Information Strategy, Dec 1998/Jan 1999, p.26
20 Crook C, Strategic Planning in the Contemporary World, American Programmer, March 1996, p.9
21 McGrath R and MacMillan I, Discovery Driven Planning, Harvard Business Review, July-August 1995, p.44
22 Stacey R, Dynamic Strategic Management for the 1990s, *(see under Bibliography)*
23 Christensen C, The Innovator's Dilemma, *(see under Bibliography)*

Appendix 1 A corporate change scenario

Introduction

Let us assume that your organisation wishes to match the requirements laid out in Chapter 12, i.e. it intends to formally adopt a more flexible, fast-changing approach to future IT development programs. This appendix will lay out one possible action-plan for changing the current corporate outlook, culture, structure and knowledge level to meet this new requirement. Note that this is no instant solution, it will always take more than a year to implement such a program.

Objectives

The activities outlined in Table A1.1 will potentially prepare the organisation for a radical change in the way system development is undertaken. In other words, it says nothing about the actual development program itself, but will only address the framework of in-house skills and requiried facilities that should be present in the organisation.

Assumptions

In what follows, the numbers will be in weeks and the corporate units involved will be: SM (senior management); BF (business functions); HR (human resource); IT (information technology), MS (management services);

Quality; and Training. The roles carried out will be principally associated with:

- ❏ BF   Sales, marketing, buying, accounts

- ❏ HR   Provision of required management skills

- ❏ IT   System development, maintenance and upgrades

- ❏ MS   Audits, risk management, change control

- ❏ Quality Test facilities, standards and documentation criteria

- ❏ Training Technical and non-technical learning programs

In terms of size, it is assumed that the organisation has 500 or more staff with a committed and competent workforce. It is further assumed that the company in question is operating at a reasonable non-crisis level in the marketplace and has some spare funds available for strategic investment.

Model project overview

The model time plan is given in Table A1.1 and is primarily intended as a base-line for further thought. Only the key activities of the first year have been outlined, even though the project would probably go on for another 25 or so weeks. The format is reasonably standard with built-in reviews (where the senior management have every opportunity to cancel any further expenditure) and regular audits (for quick discovery if something is wrong). What is not shown is the sheer workload that such a transition would call up and the corresponding resource allocation that would be needed to implement it. It will probably take about 18 months in all to get all the training exercises completed; to get the updated test equipment installed; to write the new system test procedures; to establish the new standards and documentation; and to operate under the new management structure.

If some form of this project is undertaken, it will be stressful, slow and expensive. But the odds are that it will be the only way to make this book obsolete.

Table A1.1 A timetable for transition

Deliverable	Content	Source	Time
Decision	Go for first evaluation	SM	t = 0
Report	Scope of overall corporate activity	all units	4
Decision	Go for feasibility	SM	6

Report
Audit
	Cost estimates
	Audit of current facilities
	         training capabilities
	         IT abilities
	         skill levels
		IT, MS
		all units
		Training
		IT
		HR
			9
			9
			9
			9
			9

Decision	Go for pilot proposals	SM	11
Report	Full definition corporate objectives (e.g. s'ware/methodology/HR/quality/ budgets/services/external interfaces)	all units	17
Decision	Go for start-up pilot implementation	SM	20
Manuals	Deliver first training material (SM/IT/Quality/MS)	Training	25
Courses	Start SM/IT/Quality/MS lectures	Training	26
Report	Satisfy new organisational requirements	HR	30
Audit Report	Carry out first quarterly audit Requirements for system test facilities	MS Quality	33 33
Audit Report	Carry out second quarterly audit Half-yearly progress statement	MS all units	46 46
Decision	Go for continued implementation	SM	50

Notes on Table A1.1:

❏ The key report is the combined specification of need – week 17;

❏ The key decision is the 'pilot approval' – week 20;

❏ Actual project related spend only begins after approval in week 20;

❏ The items indicate the type of inputs but the table is not complete.

Appendix 2 Some basic definitions

Components

This looks like the future path for new system strategies. But, as usual, it may take some time for a formal interface standard and a set of development techniques to be established.

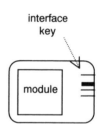

Figure A2.1
Component block

Components, also sometimes labelled 'Distributed Components' (DC) or 'Business Objects' (BO), take the concept of 'objects' (see the related section) a stage further in offering the possibility of 'don't make - buy'. In other words, standard software components with standardised interfaces could potentially be purchased from any supplier and plugged in to the system for immediate application. No in-house coding required. At the simplest level, components can be characterised by:

❏ A block of code that implements a specific software module;

❏ A 'key' that locks the component into some common interface.

At a conceptual level, the system application revolves round defining the standards and the related model that can be applied to the client server architecture. One possible format is given below:

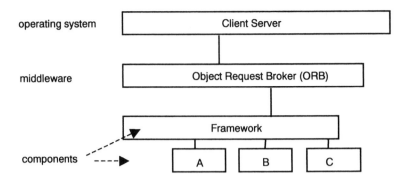

Figure A2.2 The component architecture

This structure reduces the component to the smallest and simplest level – just the function and a key. The key fits into the framework layer (one example, the 'business object facility' proposed by the OMG group) which in turn interfaces with the stardard object request broker - currently related to either the CORBA or DCOM standard - see the glossary at the end of this section.

As an example, the overall operating system could be a NOS (Network Operating System) or NT, the middleware an ORB interface based on CORBA, the framework could be a form of spreadsheet function and the individual components, perhaps, a chart generator and a font manager. These components could be placed anywhere on the network and would be transparently connected via the interfaces.

The whole subject is very much more complex that the few lines given here, calls for a completely new look at the design process and is awash with new concepts and acronyms. For more thorough material see, for example, *'Building Business Objects'*, by P. Eeles and O. Sims, (Wiley, 1998).

Glossary of terms

CORBA   Common Object Request Broker Architecture. A standard for ORBs. This standard defines the properties of the interface bus for all components linked up to it.

DCOM   Distributed Component Object Model. The Microsoft version of CORBA.

OMG   Object Management Group. A consortium of major companies that has come together to generate a standard for middleware – CORBA.

ORB   Object Request Broker. The interface bus, conforming to the appropriate standard – such as DCOM, linking all components with the same 'key'.

UML   Unified Modelling Language. A modelling tool, adopted and promoted by OMG, which can be used to capture and define the system under review.

Failure

If there are nine people in a room there will be ten definitions of 'failure'. For our purposes, the following set of definitions can be taken as a reasonable representation of the concept as applied to an IT system:

❏ Engineering. The material approach. The definition of success or failure may be mechanically expressed through measurements of some designated and testable parameters.

   Thus, one arbitrary set of figures could be:

	Success	Acceptable	Failure
Budget	< target	1.2 x target	> 1.6 x
Schedule	< target	1.2 x targ et	> 1.4 x
Performance	> spec.	0.85 x spec.	< 0.5 x

❏ Impact. Only human individuals and groups perceive intangibles such as 'disappointment', or 'anger'. In this context, failure may be expressed by some measure of dissatisfaction shown by the parties some time after the delivery of the system. In this case, one set of possible monitors could be:

	Success	Acceptable	Failure
Invoice	paid	85% paid	20% paid
Legal action	none	letters	court action
Client staff	full use	negotiation	industrial action
Installed usage	2 years	2 quarters	2 weeks

❑ Financial. The 'bottom-line' approach. If it would have been cheaper not to have developed the software system in the first place, then it is reasonable to assume that the system is a failure. This is a functional criterion, but it does pre-suppose that both the costs of development along with the cost-savings model for the new product are agreed and established - an assumption often open to question.

Maintenance

Opinions vary, but the best estimates are that maintenance will cost an organisation 50% or more of the total costs for the development of a given system. One reason for this is that any change to the existing system, as delivered to the client and currently operational, will tend to call up a complete redesign cycle to implement the change. In any case, anything exceeding 50% of the total budget outlay must call for a little respect.

Maintenance Any additional work carried out on the system structure *after* it has been formally handed over to the end-user organisation.

There are three main types of work involved: error fixing or code debugging; modifications; and upgrades.

Debugging Carrying out additional work on the system to enable it to meet the original specification as defined. Generally the responsibility of the development team.

Modifications Redesigning the system performance to meet external changes. If the sales tax or VAT requirement is modified, then the system software will have to reflect that change.

Upgrades   Enhancing the system with features that were not part of the
                    original specifications, but are now seen to be desirable by
                    the end-user. Clearly the client organisation's responsibility.

It is worth stressing that this maintenance work will continue to be
carried out for the operational life of the system. The cost-effective approach
for handling system maintenance is indicated below:

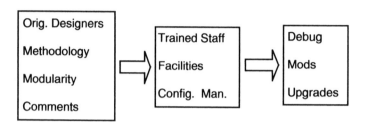

Figure A2.3 Maintenance

The left-hand box contains the main elements to be supplied by the
developers, i.e. availability of original design staff for consultation (if
possible), strongly structured design, breakdown of software into well-
defined modules and regular use of comments to describe every few lines of
code statements.

The middle box of indicates the need for specialist maintenance staff and
the proper facilites for carrying out the work. The last requirement for
efficient maintenance is the in-house utilisation of a Configuration
Management tool. This will store all the different variants of the product, the
plans, the coding and the documentation. Then new personnel can review
the existing design in order to optimise any proposed new modification.

Methodology

At the simplest level, a methodology is a set of rules for the development of
software systems. It comprises a formal collection of procedures, techniques
and tools which should enable the system developers to produce a new
system in an effective and timely manner.

It may have a number of different objectives (and these will vary from product to product). Examples could be:

❑ To enable ongoing project-related decisions between the development partners to be effectively managed;

❑ To provide a system package within specified time and cost limits;

❑ To produce a fully documented and maintainable system.

However, it is not just a 'recipe' or list of sequential activities. There will be an underlying philosophical view which will affect the nature and contents of a given methodology. There are many methodologies on the market and they vary considerably in basic approach. Thus:

❑ It may be rigidly structured, e.g. SSADM;

❑ It may be completely user centred, e.g. ETHICS;

❑ It may seek to be a mix of the two, e.g. SSM;

❑ It may reject the classical formalised approach, e.g. RAD.

The selection of methodology will have a significant impact and will be one of the more critical decision in the system development programme.

Object Oriented development

The OO technology is a radically different way of meeting software objectives and design processes. It is still a minority interest, but has become more popular over the 80s and 90s in order to satisfy two main criteria:

❑ The need to handle more data types. The conventional system approach was/is relatively weak on processing non-tabulated data such as photographs or sound bites, etc. OO technology has no such restrictions;

❑ The need for fast design. Increasingly, the demand is for month-related project times rather than year-related design cycles, and OO processes could potentially meet this requirement.

On the other hand, there is a steep learning curve, new design tools and test strategies, lack of standards and the need to change the overall development culture of the organisation. Competence across all the different development disciplines could easily cost 2 years and millions of pounds/dollars. Take this route, but with all due care.

Some definitions

Object   Everyone has their own pet view. For now, assume that a programming object-module comprises a 'class' - i.e. general grouping - and its 'instance' or sub-type.

Object examples – class: educator; instance: lecturer.

Message   Requests for action from an object (the object contains 'methods' which are the responses to specific messages).

Message examples: lecture; set_paper; mark_exam.

Inheritance   Each object will have 'properties', some of which are passed down from its class (inheritance), and some of which are unique to the specific object.

Inheritance example: Economics lecturers will inherit the 'educate' and 'lecture' property (as well as have the unique 'teach Economics' property).

Reuse   The capability to reuse software modules or objects. Much touted, but not really relevant till you have about five years design programming under your belt.

Standards

Not in good shape. This is perhaps the weakest part of the argument to go over to OO design. At the time of writing, there are no universal standards for interconnecting objects and communicating between modules. Just different proposals from different suppliers.

Programming Language

There are specific programming languages that are particularly suited to OO development and the most popular are 'Smalltalk' and 'C++'. However, learning hands-on coding and testing will take time to become proficient.

RAD

Rapid Application Development is a recent, more controlled technique which has evolved from prototyping. In broad principle, RAD is a philosophical approach to dramatically reducing system development time in a reliable and cost-effective way. It consists of some strategic (i.e. common-sense) guidelines and a set of technical core disciplines. The guidelines:

❑ Avoid classic mistakes;

❑ Apply development fundamentals;

❑ Manage risk to avoid catastrophic situations;

❑ Provide continuous liaison between the developer and the client.

And the main technical core requirements:

❑ Prototyping as the principal user/developer interface;

❑ Only a specific number of iterations allowed;

❑ Full set of 4GL tools;

❑ Timeboxing: a pre-determined time limit for each activity.

The flowchart:

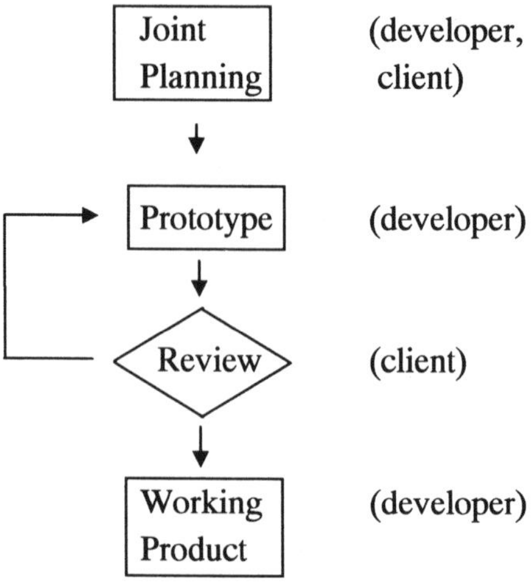

Joint Planning	(developer, client)
Prototype	(developer)
Review	(client)
Working Product	(developer)

Figure A2.4 One form of the RAD Life Cycle

The last two points above address some of the key problems with prototyping. The basic life cycle for RAD is simpler that SDLC and, like prototyping, has one fundamental difference – there is feedback during the design phase where the client may accept or reject the model shown on the screen.

By virtue of its short timescale and client interaction, it has become a popular methodology, but it still requires a lot of professionalism and care.

SEI/CMM

The letters stand for 'Software Engineering Institute/Capability Maturity Model'. It recognises that different methodologies (q.v.) on their own will not materially affect the system development process – what is needed is a root and branch change in the organisation itself. This assumes that a software development process that can be more rigorously controlled and managed will generate operational systems in a more effective manner. SEI has defined five major levels of organisational maturity which will enable such processes to be undertaken more effectively by the organisation. The attached diagram is the standard format proposed by SEI and this defines each phase or level of improvement As the company moves up these levels so the process control will progressively improve and the team will deliver progressively better systems.

It is not a simple decision, it will not suit a short timescale, it is not cheap on initial outlay, planning or culture – but it does offer the potential of successful projects some time in the future. 'Potential', but not 'certainty': making the investment, undertaking the risk and ultimately succeeding is still very much up to you.

Initial   The usual standard corporate shambles where planning is limited, tools ineffectual and change uncontrolled. This is where most organisations are currently situated.

Repeatable   Basic project management tools have been introduced where quality assurance and change control functions are now operational. However, new tools, products and objectives still constitute high-risk exercises.

Defined   Processes have now been formally documented and standardised across the organisation. Procedures will be in place to handle problems and crises in development.

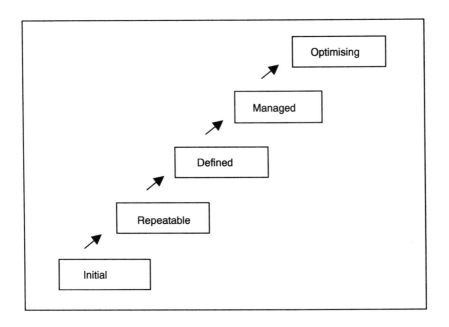

Figure A2.5 Process maturity control

Managed   Data (process parameter measurements from previous and existing projects) is now collected and reviewed on a regular basis.

Optimising   This is the final stage, where feedback to the development process itself is possible. In other words, fine tuning the process to the needs of the organisation can be achieved.

Software change sensitivity

This section will try to explain (briefly) why application systems are relatively sensitive to any form of change or modification. Such changes, even simple changes, can generate a huge amount of rework, cost and delay in any project under development or already in operational form.

To understand the nature of the problem, let us assume that a UK national retail food outlet has established a web-based grocery order plus delivery service called 'E-Retail'. The system is operational, but the main board feels that it would offer a useful marketing advantage to add Euro currency handling to the system capability. They further feel that the requirement is quite simple and the added workload will be fairly trivial. So let's investigate the nature of this 'trivial workload'.

Data

The data storage structure will have to be modified, by entering the Euro conversion rate daily. The system analysis will review how to upgrade the existing data set in the simplest possible manner using a model tool for capturing the data requirements. This tool, the *Entity Relation Diagram*, (ERD) is displayed here with the required extension shown in grey.

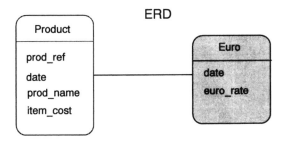

Figure A2.6 Entity relation diagram

Process

The next step is to establish how the organisation will handle data. This is analysed with another modelling tool called the Data Flow Diagram (DFD) which identifies how every element of data is treated and modified as it moves throught the various commercial sections and departments of the company. Again, one version of the tool is illustrated here.

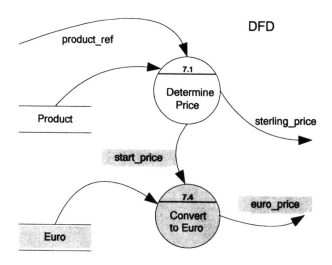

Figure A2.7 The data flow diagram

In the top part of the diagram, the product price is generated by the process 'Determine Price'. (The circle symbol indicates that the existing data is to be modified in some way – and this modification, the process, is usually described by the actual text label in the circle.). To achieve this, the 'product_ref' data is sent from some previous part of the DFD and the current item_cost for that product is derived from the data store 'Product'. The added process is shown at the bottom of the diagram again in shaded format. The 'Euro' data store (transformed here from the entity in the ERD) will supply data to the new process which in turn will deliver the required output information to the next section of the DFD.

Programming

Yet another conversion or *mapping* from the data in the previous model to the next process needs to be carried out. For software modules, one model generator is the *Jackson Structured Programming* (JSP) drawing where all programming activities are encapsulated by just three functions: sequence, iteration and selection. The related drawing is given below with the added material shown shaded. There is not an exact 1:1 mapping between the DFD and the JSP diagrams – which is why some conversion skill is needed.

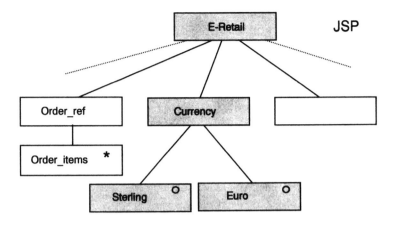

Figure A2.8 Jackson's structured programming

Once the diagram is acceptable, each of the elements can be created as lines of software code using the appropriate programming language. Here an additional module, 'currency', with its two sub-modules, will need to be coded, debugged and documented. This small block will enable either Sterling or the Euro currency to be selected by the user. Note that the upper block 'E-Retail' will also need to be modified to provide an interface to the new module.

Test

Now that the new modification has been designed and implemented, it has to be tested. There are four main test cycles: the actual module itself, i.e. 'Currency'; followed by tests with increasing degrees of integration. The last test program will be with the application upgraded at the client's site and operating in the working environment.

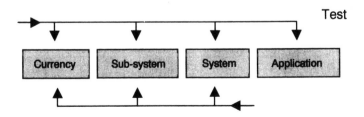

Figure A2.9 The test cycles

Each one of these test sequences will need to be documented, the test facilities set up to meet the new requirements and the test results audited and accepted. In the event that one test is not satisfactory, then the bottom line in the diagram (retest) will have to be followed. Thus, if the 'system' test fails, then you will have to return to the 'sub-system' tests to find the reason for the unacceptable performance.

Documentation

The whole exercise will carry an enormous overhead in terms of documentation generation and upgrade. Each of the system specifications will have to be modified to include the new 'currency' requirements; each of the modelling tools will have to redesign and redraw the system model; each module of new sofware code will need to be commented, documented and signed off; each of the test requirements will have to be formalised with new documents; and an entire new level of configuration control codes will have to be entered into the administrative system.

Summary

This is not a technical book, and no effort has been made to explain in depth the operations of the tools covered here. (For an introduction, try 'Software System Development' given in the bibliography.) However, even the most 'hands-off' of managers should be able to appreciate the number of steps involved in upgrading a system, the level of skills involved and the sheer workload that will be needed for the smallest system upgrade.

System

Most people know what *they* mean by the term 'system', but, for all that, understandings may vary. The general purpose definition and graphical representation are both given below.

System   A group of related elements or activities which work together to achieve some common goal. Another way of describing the function of a system is the conversion of the 'input' (whatever it is) via a 'process' to the delivered 'output' product.

Figure A2.10 The basic system

For Information Technology purposes, the fundamental process is the conversion of raw data into information which will enable decisions to be made. This process will be assisted with the control facility (checking the correct operation of the system) and the capability to store and retrieve data in the related database.

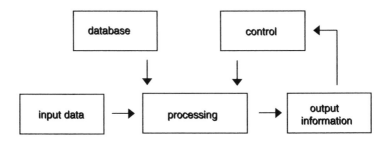

Figure A2.11 The information system

This is the basis of all IT systems in commercial application. For example, you might have a Stock_Control system. In a simplified form, this would probably have data relating to Suppliers (sources of the stored products), maybe Clients (organisations who deal with you, purchasing your finished goods), and certainly Product_Inventory (list of all parts, with their corresponding part numbers, numbers of items currently held, and their location in the warehouse). The input to the system might be a call-off order by your manufacturing division to meet a current customer order. This call-off will send the numbers held on certain parts below a critical ('re-order') level. The system will process this input (modify the existing data on Product_Inventory and alert the purchasing department to the need for re-ordering). The output could be a new purchase order to the supplier. Every so often, the quality department will send in a dummy order to check that the system is performing as expected (the control block).

If an error is seen to occur, corrective modifications to the system will be called for. In turn, you can look up the previous section to see just what is involved in applying these corrective modifications to a software system design, however small the change.

Bibliography

Strategies for Human Resource Management
Armstrong, M (Ed.)   Kogan Page 1992
A good overview of the modern approach to what used to be 'personnel'. However, not too much on the use of independent staff such as consultants, short-term contractors or facilitity management organisations.

Understanding System Failures
Bignell, V and Fortune, J   Manchester University Press 1984
A book that seeks to analyse some of the disasters, great and small, of this century. Some effort is made to provide an underlying explanation in each case.

Software System Development - A Gentle Introduction
Britton C and Doake J   McGraw-Hill 1993
The ideal reader for non-technical managers or end-users involved in the technical development of commercial software systems. Clearly and accurately written.

The Mythical Man-Month
Brooks, F   Addison-Wesley 1995
The definitive book on bringing common-sense into the software project industry. It is as valid today as when first written in the mid-70s.

Crash
Collins T and Bicknell D   Simon and Schuster   1997
A review by leading IT investigative journalists of recent system development projects. Not a pretty sight.

The Innovator's Dilemma
Christiansen, C.M.   Harvard Business School 1997

An interesting view on how some types of technological change just cannot be handled using conventional management techniques. Backed up with some solid case study material.

On the Psychology of Military Incompetence
Dixon, N.F.   Futura Publications   1979

A survey and analysis of self-induced military catastrophes. He provides a satisfying and over-arching explanation for a number of apparently unique encounters separated widely in both space and time.

Transition to Object-Oriented Software Development
Fayad M, and Laitinen, M   Wiley 1998

Relaxed but thorough introduction to the management and project related issues of switching over to an OO system development. A good reference source.

Software Runaways
Glass, R.L.   Prentice Hall 1998

Another approachable review of total project disasters, this time US-based IT development exercises that simply never made it. It, like 'Crash', comes with a set of underlying explanations.

Great Planning Disasters
Hall, P   Penguin   1980

Another selection of non-IT related case studies that illustrate how failure can occur in general construction and engineering projects.

The Prince
Machiavelli, N   Penguin 1994

It was, of course, first published in 1532, but there are still real management lessons for the IT moguls of today. Such as - how to survive!

Rapid Development
McConnell, S   Microsoft Press 1996

Justification, advantages and need (compared to, say, SSADM) with full evaluation of its design features and application in the corporate environment.

Information Management Decisions
O'Brien, B   Pitman 1995
A refreshing insight into conventional strategic thinking. Takes on currently held
views, and usually wins. Pragmatic and aggressive – and all the better for it.

The Object-Oriented Approach
Satzinger, J. and Orvik, T.   Course Technology 1996
Another very useful introduction to the application and problem areas of OO usage.
It is short, it is non-technical, and it is well written. What more can you ask for?

Dynamic Strategic Management for the 1990s
Stacey, R.D.   Kogan Page 1991
Strongly and intelligently argued case for throwing conventional long-term planning
out of the window. Change control, it is claimed, is the only worthwhile track to
follow.

Death March
Yourdon, E   Prentice Hall 1997
An examination of survival techniques in software development projects which are
virtually bound to fail. An entertaining coverage of a very serious topic, delivered
with some gusto by one of the leading practitioners in the trade.

Software 2000: A View of the Future
A report on a workshop (with the same title) sponsored by ESPRIT and ICL
Commission of the European Communities   1994

TickIT
Guide to Software Quality Management System, Construction and Certification
The outline of a regime for becoming certified to meet BS 5750 Part 1.
Department of Trade and Industry   1990

Are Major Information Technology Projects Worth the Risk?
Establishes the nature of the risk in large IT projects using some existing examples
and puts forward recommendations to minimise that risk.
Griffiths C. and Willcocks L.   1994

Breaking the Barriers
IT Effectiveness in Great Britain and Ireland
A survey of the successful application (or not) of IT by leading UK companies.
Kearney, A.T.   1990

What Went Wrong? Unsuccessful Information Technology Projects
A survey of leading Canadian companies to establish their experience in software
project failures.
KPMG (Canada)   1997

Process Management (Optimising Software Development)
An introduction to why current methods are inadequate and how 'Process Management' could solve most of the current problems in this area.
LMBS Europe Ltd   1994

IT Security Breaches Survey Summary
A survey of the frequency and cost of mechanisms that can cause a computer installation to fail - and ways to minimise their impact.
National Computing Centre   1994 .

The Performance of Information Technology and the Role of Human and Organisational Factors
A review of the experience of 45 consultants and professional researchers, who were asked to estimate the success rate of IT projects they had worked on.
OASIG   1996

Understanding Why Systems Fail to Deliver
A survey of about a 100 UK companies. It looks at some of the reasons why systems fail to deliver and illustrates the shortcomings of current approaches.
Pagoda Consulting Ltd.   1994

Managing information and systems risks
An independent survey of directors and managers in 500 companies in 8 countries based on their experiences of using IT systems in their organisations.
PricewaterhouseCoopers   1996

Chaos (Application Project and Failure)
A comprehensive and illuminating survey of software project failure by a leading US research organisation.
The Standish Group   1995

Index 1 Case histories

Index 2 General topics